SELF-LOVE WORKBOOK FOR WOMEN

A Life-Changing Guide to Learn how to Say No, Take Care of your Body, and Change your Mind. Discover the Powerful Methods Used by Successful, Famous Women

Additionally, the information in the following pages is intended only for informational purposes and should thus be thought of as universal. As befitting its nature, it is presented without assurance regarding its prolonged validity or interim quality. Trademarks that are mentioned are done without written consent and can in no way be considered an endorsement from the trademark holder.

Introduction

We all feel down in our lives every once in a while. We do everything we can to make ourselves feel happy and comfortable with our lives. But even with all that, it is still a challenge to try and make our lives as great as they could be.

It is a necessity for all of us to think about the things we can for improving our lives and making them feel stronger and better. This guide is all about helping you to understand what you can do to give your life a greater sense of purpose.

It is especially critical for you to look into what you can do to restore your life and give your self-esteem the boost it needs. When you feel better about yourself, your life becomes a little easier. You will not try and make things all the more challenging than they have to be. You will certainly feel confident about who you are without dragging yourself down any paths that might be harmful or dangerous.

Your emotions will also be easier to control when you have the self-esteem you require. You will not feel as though you are letting yourself or other people down.

It will be easier for you to have better relationships with other people as well. The general public prefers individuals who feel positive about themselves. They want those who are ready to do anything and are not afraid of themselves.

More importantly, you will feel happier about yourself when you have enough self-esteem in your life. There is no reason why you should feel upset with your life. As you are improving upon your attitude for life, you will find that it is not all that hard for you to get the most out of your everyday experience.

Avoiding Comparisons

One of the greatest reasons why so many people struggle with their lives is because they are constantly trying to compare themselves with others. Some like to compare themselves because they want to think that they are as good as others.

It is natural for all of us to compare ourselves to other people. We all have our own heroes or idols that we love to follow. But sometimes we get far too caught up in those things. We start to think far too much about people and what they are like.

We all like to compare ourselves with all of these people because we think they are all better than us and appealing in some way.

But when we do this, we struggle to look at the big picture.

It only takes a few thoughts or observations of other people

to start getting the wrong idea over what can be done in life to make it stand out.

But the truth is that you cannot compare yourself to other people all the time. Think about it for a moment. Let us say that you like to play baseball. You want to try and build your skills up to where you can be the next big-name baseball player.

But no matter what you do, you might struggle to be a big star. You might try and work yourself to death just to try and make it onto a particular team.

It can be difficult to think about how you are not as good as baseball as other people are. That does not mean that you should be comparing yourself all the time.

Not everyone who plays baseball can hit a ball as hard as Aaron Judge. Most certainly cannot throw a ball as fast as Max Scherzer can. They might not be able to make the smartest managerial decisions like Mike Matheny or Joe Madden could.

More importantly, you will feel as though you are not willing to let yourself be who you truly are if you compare yourself to others all the time.

You will not feel all that comfortable with who you are in general when you keep on comparing yourself with others in some way.

Simply put, you have to stop comparing yourself to other people all the time. Everyone has their strengths. You just need to think about yours.

Look at Your Strengths

When you work to improve your life, you have to think about your strengths. Look at what you do for a living and think about how you might excel in certain things.

Everyone has skills that make them great at something. Some people might be talented writers who have a way with words. Others can fix up all sorts of vehicles.

Look at the strengths you have and see what you can do to build upon them or to use them to your advantage. If you are good with cars, then maybe you could consider working at a vehicle repair shop. Maybe you could go to a technical education program to learn how to work with commercial vehicles or high-end vehicles from Maserati or Ferrari, among others. The potential for you to go far with your skills is endless when you know what you are great at or when you build upon those abilities.

Think about those strengths that you have in your life and see what you can do to move forward with them. You might be surprised when you think about what you are good at and work on those things in particular.

As you look at those strengths, you will be free to be who you truly are. You will not be limited to trying to be like someone you are not. Instead, you are blazing your trail as you stick with those positives. It makes your life all the more worthwhile when considered right.

Focus on Being Good Enough

You should not assume that you have to be perfect in everything you do in your life. Perfection is something that no one can ever truly accomplish.

Rather, you should think about being good enough for whatever it is you are doing. Look at how you are working on your goals and how you are moving closer to completing them.

For instance, you might have a desire to be a car technician. You could study at a vocational school and complete your tests to be certified. After this, you would find a great job with a quality repair shop or another place that could use your services.

Do not think that you have to be perfect in every aspect of your work. Instead, think more about what you can do to pass your exams. Look at how you are going to work on different vehicles at the start of your career.

You have to think less about perfection and more about what is coming in the here and now. When you complete your exams and find a job, you will see that you truly are good enough to be where you want to be.

Of course, you can use this as a steppingstone to a much greater objective like working for a distinct group or taking care of unique cars that might be a little fancier. But whatever the case is, everything you do must be done gradually without forcing yourself into situations that might be too tough to get into.

Keeping your life organized and in check can truly be helpful. Be certain when looking at your life that you think carefully about how well you are not likely to lose control of it all.

Avoid thinking that everything has to work as well as possible. Focus more on being positive with your life while looking at what you could do to move forward in any manner.

More importantly, avoiding perfection is critical in that reality can get in the way of this concept. You might think you have to do things in a certain way, but in reality, you would end up having problems happen that cause you to think bad things.

As you stick with a better mindset, you will find that your life is indeed worthwhile. You will not be a slave to your own mind as you start to get on your way to happiness. More importantly, you will not feel as though you cannot go anywhere in your life.

Be ready to think for yourself. It makes a world of difference when you see what makes your life stand out and powerful.

Chapter 1 How Famous Women Who Have Had Disadvantages in Their Lives Have Managed to Overcome Obstacles! What Principles Did They Use?

According to Emma Watson, self-care is all about self-love. Most of us find it very hard to love and accept our own self. I want you to understand that you can never truly love and accept another person without loving and accepting yourself first.

If you do not agree with this, then think about it again. Is there someone in your life whom you love immensely? How do you feel about them? Do you like everything about them or do you feel that they would be perfect if only some things would change? Most likely, you want to change some things about them even though you know that they will most likely never change (at least, not until they decide to change which is something you have very little control over).

The sun does not compare itself with the moon, a rose does not compare itself with a marigold, a skylark does not compare itself with a nightingale. There is room enough for all of us to be amazing without stepping on each other's shoes.

Let the inner love flow towards your own heart. After that, you will have ample compassion to offer to others. Your example will inspire others to love and accept their own self. You will be a beacon of love and beauty in this world. Hence, be gentle and compassionate towards yourself. You are your own greatest responsibility.

Deepen Your Relationship with Yourself

Which is the most important relationship in the world?

Whether you currently realize this or not – the most important relationship in the world is the one that you have with your own Self. How you relate with your own Self sets the ground for how others relate to you.

The outer world is only a mirror to your inner reality. The relationships you have with other people are, in some way, a reflection of the relationship you have with yourself.

Do you like yourself? Do you love yourself unconditionally? Do you see the good in yourself? Or do you constantly beat yourself up for the flaws that you think you possess?

I have said it before, and I will say it again. Accepting and loving yourself unconditionally is the very foundation of a life of self-care.

Even if no one has said this to you yet – I am going to say this to you today, and you better start believing it! You are beautiful, you are amazing, you are gorgeous – you deserve the best that life has to offer. There never was, never has been, and never will be another one exactly like you in this world or in any other. You must reclaim your power and your gifts from the Universe by acknowledging the limitlessness of your soul and the inherent beauty of your individuality.

Get past the scarcity mindset by ceasing to compare yourself with others. You can only be the protagonist of your own story and your story is just as unique as you are. When you compare yourself with others you fail to realize that your only competition is with your own self. As long as you are striving to constantly grow and become a better person than who you were yesterday, you are living the true potential of your soul.

There is room enough for all of us to be gorgeous, amazing, and superbly brilliant. Which flower ever craves to be like another one? Yet, each flower is so incredibly beautiful in its own unique way. If you go to any natural place, you will realize that nature is all about harmony and co-existence. The wind is not competing with the water. The sun is not competing with the moon. The forest is not competing with the desert.

Nature has so many varieties, yet every element present in it is unique and beautiful in its own way. There is no competition. Human beings are also meant to be the same way. Each of us is a diamond shining with its own distinctive luster and brightness.

From now on, put a full stop on all comparisons, and start relishing your own individuality. There just cannot be another you.

Never forget that the secret to stop comparing yourself with others is to love and accept yourself unconditionally. The more you are in love with yourself, the less chances there will be of you wanting to compare yourself with anyone else.

This week, I want you to be watchful of your internal talk with yourself – start noticing all the self-sabotaging thoughts/activities you indulge in. A life of self-care requires you to shed your true self in all its magnificent glory without being weighed down by any excess baggage.

We are usually very hard on ourselves. If only we could see ourselves from the eyes of those who love and admire us, it would not be so difficult to accept our own inherent perfection.

No matter what you believe about yourself, trust me you are a far more amazing person than you think you are.

How easy or hard has been for you to love and accept yourself unconditionally so far? If you are like most people, then this has likely not been an easy journey for you. You might be struggling with crippling self-doubt, constant self-abnegation, and instant self-criticism.

I just want to tell you that no matter where you are in your journey right now, things ARE GOING TO START LOOKING UP if you only persist with this course and continue doing what you must do to get to your goal of effortless self-care and boundless self-love.

Now, let me ask you something: What do you do when you are in love with someone?

You give them all your attention and spend as much time as you possibly can with them. Isn't it?

Have you been spending any time with yourself without constantly looking for distractions so that you do not have to face the voice within your own head? Today I want to urge you to spend time with yourself. Dare to be alone with no one but your own self for company. No matter how uncomfortable this makes you, I want you to do it and I want you to start from today. Also remember that growth starts at the end of our comfort zone. Greatness is not achieved by living a comfortable life – it is achieved by constantly moving out of our comfort zone to face new challenges that compel us to raise our standards and hold up our own self to a new much higher one.

You become the person that you believe you are. If you believe you are smart and beautiful, that is what you will eventually become. If you believe you are a loser who cannot do anything right, then that is the reality you will create for yourself. And by believing, I do not mean what you think of yourself or try to think of yourself in your conscious mind. I mean what you truly believe to be true for yourself within your subconscious mind.

The people around you simply mirror your own beliefs about yourself. You are constantly emitting thought vibrations about what you believe to be true for yourself. Any person who comes in contact with your aura picks up these vibrations and starts treating you the way you think you deserve to be treated.

Have you ever noticed how on those days when you look in the mirror and say, "I'm looking very good today," you end up receiving a lot of compliments? Then, there are those days when you look in the mirror and say, "I look awful. I'm a total mess." On that day, it seems like every other person is reaffirming this idea to you.

Eliminate Clutter and Create an Inspiring Space

Clutter not only affects the aesthetics of your outer environment but also the beauty of your inner space. Just try meditating in a room that has dirty laundry strewn around and you will know what I mean. It will not be too far-fetched to say that your environment is your mind. You just cannot think clearly enough as long as you have untidiness surrounding you.

This week, I would like you to eliminate clutter from your life. Eventually, I want you to work on both your inner and your outer environment. To get started, we will focus on the outer clutter.

I would suggest that you start identifying what is truly important to you. Begin the decluttering process by removing everything that you do not use anymore or that is broken and non-functional.

Say YES to Life!

We all have these things that we keep putting off for 'someday.' Someday we would wear our favorite dress, join the ballet class, learn piano, take out that fine China for dinner and what not. Yet the only time we have is this present moment.

A lot of people reach the end of their earthly life feeling like they never got a chance to be truly alive. There is nothing worse than regret. Tomorrow you will regret everything you did not do today.

Also, when you constantly put off living until tomorrow, you never end up fully appreciating all the gifts that you have today.

In order to completely embrace life and make the most of it in the here and now, you must show up at your best. Wear your best clothes, use your fine china for meals, do what you really want to do on a daily basis as if today was the last day of your life (because one day you are going to be right about it). When death comes, most people do not regret the mistakes they made as much as they regret the time that they lost which they could have spent in being truly alive.

Learning to Say NO

Just like saying 'Yes' to life is important, saying 'NO' at the right time and place is equally important. A lot of times we say 'yes' to the wrong things for the wrong reasons. Usually, this happens when we do not want to disappoint the other person. We make a compromise with our own wishes and say yes to something that does not feel good to our heart.

The problem with this is that even though you end up looking good to the other person, you are letting your own self down. You are bound to feel resentful and also angry (most likely) towards yourself and towards that person.

It is very important to know who you are as a person, what your values are, what you are okay with, and what you are not okay with. This will help you set powerful boundaries. Not having boundaries will constantly make you feel as if you are being pushed in different directions by other people. Taking a firm stand for yourself is necessary for living a happy and fulfilling life.

Chapter 2 The Equation of Self-Love. What Are the Principles That Make Us Love Ourselves?

Self-Compassion & Your Emotions

Why We Feel What We Feel

EMOTIONS ARE UNIVERSAL. We are all born equipped to feel a range of emotional experiences, from the elation of joy to the hopelessness of despair. Emotions bring color and intensity to our everyday experiences, and if we pay attention, they can provide us with important information on how we are experiencing things moment to moment. Our strongest emotions—like love—can give our lives meaning and purpose. However, emotions can also be challenging and, at times, quite painful. All too often we fall into the habit of judging ourselves for having certain feelings, such as fear or vulnerability. It is also common to try to avoid unpleasant feelings, and in so doing, we cause ourselves even more pain.

Emotions serve an important purpose in that they help us interpret our experiences and successfully navigate the world. Anxiety, happiness, and excitement can highlight and guide us toward what matters and also let us know if a given situation or interaction is going well or not. Do we feel confident? Threatened? Bored? Anxious? When we tune in to our emotions, we find a wealth of crucial information.

We have many different types of emotions that function to help us in different ways. For example, we experience:

→Emotions that signal threat or danger: anger, fear, or disgust.

→Emotions that alert us to losses or disappointments: sadness, remorse, or grief.

→Emotions that show us things we like, or want to achieve or acquire excitement, desire, anticipation, and joy.

→Emotions that help us feel soothed, safe, and connected: contentment and calm.

We also can and often do experience more than one emotion in any given moment. A single event or experience can bring up a range of emotions, which sometimes makes understanding and responding to our emotions challenging. For instance, going on a first date might cause a mixture of happiness and anxiety, while making a mistake at work might evoke anxiety, anger, and possibly even sadness. Each evoked emotion comes with different sensations, thoughts, and motivations. When we experience a mix of emotions, it can sometimes feel like they are pulling us in different directions.

If we can learn to approach our emotions with self-compassionate awareness and understanding, we are more likely to be able to experience our emotions without being ruled by them. Self-compassionate approaches to emotions allow us to accept, understand, and respond to our emotional experiences in a helpful way. This can prevent our feelings from randomly taking over our actions and essentially running our lives.

Getting Centered

To prepare for engaging with your emotions, you will begin with a primary practice that lays the foundation for much mind-body work: centering rhythmic breathing. Variations of this practice are used in many forms of compassion training, from ancient yogic meditations, to Tibetan Buddhist visualizations, to modern psychotherapy techniques. In fact, rhythmic breathing exercise is a foundational practice in Compassion Focused Therapy, a type of therapy developed by Paul Gilbert. This initial exercise in training the mind in compassion is directly related to cultivating self-compassionate awareness and attention and will be the first step on your path to self-compassion. The aim here is to learn to center your awareness, slowing down your mind and body. This frees you to focus your attention on accessing compassionate awareness. From this grounding in mindful compassion, you can truly pay attention to what is going on here and now.

CENTERING RHYTHMIC BREATHING

Find a comfortable and quiet place to sit. Sit upright, with a straight but relaxed spine, so you can breathe comfortably and deeply. Feel free to adjust your posture at any time to remain in a comfortable and open position throughout this practice.

Allow your eyes to close and bring your awareness to your breath. Let your attention gently rest on each inhalation and exhalation. Notice the gentle rise of your chest or belly when breathing in. Notice the gentle fall of your chest or belly as you breathe out. Feel yourself letting go. Simply allow yourself to notice the sensations of breathing.

Your mind will wander. It is what minds do. When you notice this happening, gently bring your awareness back to your experience of breathing.

With your next inhalation, see if you can allow your breath to gradually slow, extending the in-breath and allowing it to be slower, deeper, and longer. As much as you can, breathe slowly, smoothly, and evenly. Feel the in-breath for a count of four to five seconds, hold for a moment, and release the out-breath for four to five seconds. Take a few moments to experiment to find a pace that feels right.

Stay with the even, slow rhythm. Focusing on the full experience of the slow, even in-breath and slow, even out-breath, rest your awareness in the act of breathing, holding yourself in kindness, for a few moments longer.

Before you open your eyes, give yourself some credit for taking time to practice caring for yourself in this way. Next, expand your awareness, feeling your feet on the floor, your weight supported by the chair or ground, your open posture. When you are ready, at your own pace, open your eyes, exhaling and letting go of this practice.

Self-Compassion & Your Body

OUR EXPERIENCES OF THE WORLD AROUND US and the way our bodies feel are closely connected. However, because we are not always consciously aware of how we feel physically, we can easily overlook how much the state of our bodies influences things like our mood, motivation level, and the lens through which we perceive what is happening to us. Too often, instead of being nurtured, our bodies are ignored, neglected, or wind up being the focus of self-criticism. Increasing self-compassion also involves learning to cultivate awareness and paying better attention to our physical selves. Compassionate understanding of the impact your physical experience has on your life can lead to a new appreciation of your body, its rhythms, and its needs. Self-compassionate motivation and action can help you find ways to be more helpful and kind to the body that works so hard for you every day.

Noticing Your Bodily Experiences

Awareness and attention are the first steps in bringing self-compassion to your body. A good way to begin is by paying attention to how your body is feeling here and now, and how you might be responding to those feelings. Just like you practiced with your emotions, you will learn to notice and attend to how your body is functioning, your posture, your physical feelings, and the experiences of your senses. With this next exercise, I invite you to take a few moments to check in with how your body is feeling right now.

NOTICING PHYSICAL SENSATIONS & EXPERIENCES

Close your eyes and take a few slow, even breaths, or engage in centering rhythmic breathing. After you have centered your attention with your breath, bring your focus to your body. Take a brief inventory. What do you notice about your body temperature? What do you notice about your muscle tension? Do you notice any sensations of touch? Hearing? Smell? Simply allow yourself to note any and all felt experiences of your body, here and now.

When you are ready, open your eyes and get your notebook. It is time to write down some of your observations and reflections, using the following questions to guide you:

→Body temperature: Are you warm, hot, cold, or cool? If so, where do you notice this?

→Muscles: Are you tense or tight? Are you relaxed? If so, where do you notice this?

→Other sensations: What else are you feeling in your body? Is there any tingling? Numbness? Something else?

→Additional senses: Do you hear anything? Smell anything? What about taste?

In this exercise, you may have noticed some judgmental thoughts or criticisms of your body. The new self-compassion skills you are learning are not easy, but they are even more challenging if you are judging yourself. Self-compassion helps us become more aware of our physical experiences without judging them. Once we are more able to tune in to how our bodies are feeling with compassionate awareness and attention, we can determine how to take good care of ourselves. Next, we will look at the different ways you might be judging your body and find alternative responses to your bodily experiences.

How Are You Judging Your Body?

Many of us treat our bodies as rivals rather than allies. We view the physical sensations and bodily functioning as a source of constant dissatisfaction or disappointment, and the subject of our criticism and judgment. Struggling against unwanted sensations or focusing on how our bodies do not look or perform the way we want them to, leads to unnecessary distress.

Taking a judgmental approach toward our bodies can lead to shame and self-criticism, as well as problematic behaviors like avoidance, denial, or attempts to control our bodies in unhelpful ways like excessive dieting. While we cannot—and should not—avoid or deny the fact that we will not always like our bodily experiences, we can learn to respond in kinder ways. As you cultivate compassion for your body, you will be better equipped to respond more effectively to discomfort or distress.

Chapter 3 Why Be Inspired by Women Who Have Achieved Success with A Touch of Selfishness?

According to Emma Watson being selfish with your time and effort does not make you a bad person. Sometimes these actions protect us from the danger that is out there and for people that could use us for their own benefit.

We have to learn to say no when we actually want to say no, compromising is sometimes not needed because it makes us slaves for other people, and we forget that we need to take care of ourselves too.

When we become selfish with our time most people feel like we are anti-social but actually we are doing that to take care of ourselves. We have to learn not to be always there when wanted. Learn to be unavailable and try not to please everyone because you cannot.

How about you please yourself? How about you become selfish with your time because you also need to spend time with yourself?

It is just like effort, we keep doing stuff for people, but they do not return the favor, how about you start being selfish with your effort? How about you start pulling back and fading in the background with your efforts? Some will look at that in a bad way, remember you are doing this for yourself and not for anyone out there.

Learn to say I cannot make it when you actually cannot make it. Do not force yourself to be in environments that are not conducive for you or where you do not feel welcome. Sometimes you will be forcing yourself to fit in. It will take a lot from you; you will feel like you are disappointing everyone else, but the end results will be great. You will be happy because you are taking time to teach people that you are not always going to be there, we also need to be there for ourselves.

When people miss having you around, they start questioning if they did anything wrong sometimes, they evaluate your friendships or your relationships and they start treating you differently, it is ok the phase will pass. You will have to be ready for it and know you do not need excuses. You can be honest and tell people that you are working on yourself. Those who will pull out of the relationship you have with them were always going to go because true friends support each other. Always

Gratitude

At the end of it all we have to be thankful and show appreciation. Gratitude can change your life completely and you realize you have been so uptight, and you need to loosen up and gratitude will help you do that.

Gratitude on its own can build a person because a lot is learnt. Being nice and you look at things in a totally different way.

Start a habit of starting your mornings with words of gratitude, if you have a book or a journal every morning jot down what you're grateful for, if it's something that was done by someone, or you're just grateful for Life. You can be grateful for the family that you have or grateful for the job that you have, just write it down so that it can be a reminder that you have always said thank you when it matters.

Gratitude makes us appreciate even little things we never paid attention to and we should know that gratitude carries so much power because our emotions relate to feeling thankful and being appreciated. You are becoming a very nice person because of gratitude; you look at the things you have and be grateful that someone out there does not have them, but you are there with everything that is around you.

Even when you wake up in the morning, being grateful that you saw another dawn, a new day and someone out they did not wake up and the family is mourning. Gratitude is important but we forget it a lot during our lifetime until we go through something and it is not supposed to be like that.

Gratitude should become part of your personality trait, mood, and emotions because that is going to be a beautiful radiance of love connection with the world because gratitude can change your mentally.

Most people are not aware that being thankful can actually make one a happy person like I said it changes a person completely. Things that did not matter start being important. Those times of waking up and having little complaints than usual go away and that is what gratitude does.

Benefits of gratitude are a lot but, in this book, I just want to focus much on self-introspection like asking yourself if you have been more thankful and grateful or you have been focusing more on the negativity of life. That is when we lose it, when negativity takes over, we lose a lot of thankfulness. We start seeing everything in a negative way even when people smile at us.

Gratitude can change that, clearly you can be happy that at least in a day someone smiled at you, with so many people walking around with serious faces someone smiled at you. Gratitude encourages development of patience and humility and wisdom to the fact that now you start being positive and you are doing things differently. You start appreciating life, you become patient because impatience is one of the most negative things that you can keep around with you. Impatience can make you miss opportunities by a minute.

Humility is underrated but as much as we express it in the world and also appreciate things, people start looking at us differently when we express such humility, we carry a lot of greatness. It covers us with greatness because people start looking at us in a different way and they start seeing a different person who appreciates life and humility is also brought by being grateful.

Gratitude has been used as guidance for some people who have gone through stuff. Sometimes they are asked questions that have to do with gratitude so that they realize that even when they are going through troubles there are things, they can be grateful for.

 Right now, you have access to a book like this one that can help you, someone out there is going through a lot fighting demons by themselves and they have no one not even a material to read but here you are, reading this guide.

It is one of the things to be thankful for, you have access to tools that can help you be a better person.

Gratitude carries value that is meant to connect people with each other in a nicer way, gratitude makes you become light and life lightens up the burdens that you have carried.

You offload most of the things because you become optimistic, you are thankful for what you have, and you know tomorrow you will be thankful for beating the demos that you are fighting.

You can make gratitude a tendency because it changes things, when you make it a tendency it becomes easy, it does not become forced or you don't seek it you don't even have to remind yourself that you have to be grateful. It comes naturally even when you do your morning prayers or devotions you realize that when you start with a gratitude everything flows easily.

Even people that have done things for us and we show the sign of gratitude and we are thankful we can still go back to them and ask for help and they will always help us not because we gave them anything but because we were thankful and grateful.

So now this is the great weapon that you carry, gratitude makes you happier to be honest. Being thankful makes everyone happier, I believe so because you carry so much happiness that comes with humility. With things that are happening in your life like being late at work, sometimes when you get there you realize that no one has come but all the way you were angry with yourself because the bus left you but again you have to be grateful that you made it to work.

Chapter 4 Why in Some Circumstances Do We Have to Put Ourselves Before Everything Else First?

LOVE YOURSELF, BEFORE YOU LOVE ANOTHER

Self-love is a source of goodwill and respect. If these feelings are not enough, the relationship becomes authoritarian or is built on the type of "victim - persecutor".

Psychologists agree on one thing: self-love is an essential thing necessary in order to love other people too, and the whole world, and generally feel comfortable.

First of all, it is good for your health. Self-love is the most reliable vaccine against all sorts of psychosomatic diseases and stress prevention. One who does not love himself first uses, and then destroys the confidence of the partner. "The supplier of love" becomes embarrassed, he begins to doubt and eventually gets tired of proving his feelings. The mission is impossible: one cannot give to another that which he can give himself only, love of himself. One who does not love himself often unconsciously calls into question the feelings of another: So, he's worse than me!" The lack of self-love can also take the form of almost manic devotion, obsession with love.

Importance of self-love

Still, to see, understand, and love another, you need to understand and love yourself: Who Am I? What am I? How do I? If you learn to respond to your pain, joy, your desires, then you can respond to the feelings of another person close to you.

How to understand that it is time to transform your attitude

Consider yourself a failure? Do you think that there is nothing attractive about the opposite sex in you? All these thoughts are reflected not only on your face but also in your behavior, in your daily communication with friends, colleagues, relatives.

If a person suffers for some time in contact with others and suffers, if he does not like his own life, then it is worth thinking. But it is hardly worth it to "change yourself," but opening up yourself to the present and falling in love over again with yourself is real.

This understanding comes to different people in diverse ways. And it is all hinge on the person himself. If he thinks about why he is not valued, respected, or why someone is constantly manipulating him, then these are visible signs of dislike for himself. And you may have to do something about it.

It is time to care for ourselves, as a rule, reminds us of a state of depression when your own "I" is in the shadow of the "object" in a passive position. When there is no faith in ourselves, when we think that something good can only be thanks to the efforts of other people, and not our own. Also, the criterion that you require to heed to self-love is the absence of close and emotionally warm, stable love relationships. A person who loves himself, and not suffering from selfishness, always find a steady and fulfilling relationship, where he is loved.

Learning to love yourself

What to do, how to go about caring yourself with all the shortcomings?" - we asked psychologists. And how practically, successfully should our love for ourselves be revealed?

You can assume that you are a moms and dad to yourself. And study how to love yourself from this position - discover to feel your requirements and desires, accept errors as an experience, give yourself support, and so on. But better than dealing with a psychologist, it is not likely that you or anybody alone can do it yourself. I feel, authorize, offer myself support, look after myself, cultivate myself, do not permit the usage, and so on" - she recommends taking this mindset as a basis.

Self-love techniques

Set objectives, albeit little ones, but be sure to attain them! And whenever you reach, applaud yourself and value you for your determination, for your work, for your efforts. Appreciation influences. Avoid popular slogans like "well done."

Bear in mind that even effective business owners and acknowledged beauties-models are not without complexes. Take a little book or a paper and split it into two columns or sides. Compose your strengths on the right, on the left - what you wish to alter in yourself. If you attempt to be objective,

You will comprehend that really, there are no fewer positive qualities in you than reasons for dissatisfaction with yourself and cultivating complexes.

Self-love should, to start with, be revealed in caring for yourself. About his health, about his appearance, about the complete satisfaction of his own, and not somebody else's desires. In the necessary observance of details health - you needless to fill your brains with all sorts of negativity. Self-love is the capability to develop convenience around you - both psychological and physical.

There are individuals for whom looking after kids, family, and other individuals comprises the meaning of life. Do they have to find out to enjoy themselves more?

And it cannot truly successfully care for other people who forget about themselves. And therefore, he teaches his close ones how not to enjoy oneself. When an individual with super care takes children into a life, he is left without meaning.

Excessive care for other acts as a desire to affirm one's value, not to feel in requirement of care, but to feel strong and positive. I cannot care for myself, due to the fact that I feel shame, guilt, vulnerability ... Then I put my "child" part in another person and care for him as myself, while I can likewise permit myself to feel crucial, necessary, and almighty.

How to comprehend where the border lies, does not self-love mean common egoism? Psychologists plainly share these concepts. Selfishness is behavior that is totally determined by the idea of one's own advantage, advantage when a private puts his interests above the well-beings of others. A man who loves himself will never ever consider himself superior to others. He understands his value, respectively, understands that everyone is as important as he is. He will treat others around him with respect and love.

Preferably, when an individual really loves himself, he generously provides it to others from the excess of love inside himself.

And if one is selfish, then his love for himself will be selfish. Strictly speaking, it is more correct to talk here not about love for oneself, but about falling for oneself. The charm of oneself, self-absorption, exaggeration of one's virtues are signs of falling for oneself, and such a love is really quite selfish. If a person thinks about others and cares about them, then his love for himself is not connected with egoism in any way, it is easy and natural for him to love both himself and others. The forces for this are quite enough. Anyone who loves himself for a while and naturally does not devote too much time to this, just as a well-maintained gardener does not require too much trouble. It is easy to care of oneself to a healthy and vigorous person. Did you wake up? She raised herself sweetheart with pleasure, washed herself beautiful, was glad for herself peppy - and there is no longer much need for herself to do anything else. Everything is already great, I already want to do something or someone else: prepare a delicious breakfast for we and home, kiss everyone and help get together. The reality, however, is that those who have become preoccupied with self-love, at least initially become more selfish - just because the main focus, in this case, begins to be on their beloved. Supplementing self-love with attention and care for others is perhaps not difficult, but it is a completely separate area of work. Love for others in itself from love for itself does not follow and does not follow. One of the mysteries of self-love is in this inner joy and in its simple formula, namely: heat, light, and energy. It is fine! But sometimes it is cold in your soul, and when you feel cold in your soul, you do not have love. If a person describes a picture of his inner world as - grey, well, some winter, some evening, maybe the lights went out, and there is no joy or energy in his voice - such a person lives without love. But how to give birth and maintain light and warmth in your soul? What needs to be done for this?

People often think that self-love consists in satisfying their simplest needs with pleasure, forgetting about duties and other people. Allow yourself to explore and do what you want, allow yourself shopping, surround yourself with romance and give yourself gifts - an exciting program for a human child who does not intend to grow up. Can this be called love? It is possible, but the level of this love is the same as the love of a mother, in whom the child feeds mainly on candies and Coca-Cola, spending time mainly on computer games and other entertainments.

Strictly speaking, it is even hard to call needs. These are the desires and whims that spoiled children insist on. And the most essential thing is that they give joy, not for long, only while it is new and while others are jealous of it. After some time, everything becomes boring, the joy leaves. Sometimes a girl seemed to give herself everything: slept, watered, fed herself, and arranged for herself shopping - but inside everything is bad.

Sadly. The world is gray, and the girl is still nibbling herself for something. Does she love herself? No. It turns out that a woman is interested in shopping just because she is ill with herself. And if a woman is in some kind of insult to life, she can arrange a shopping for herself, and then she looks at these things, but there is no joy. In itself, satisfying needs is not self-love, and far from always, it ends with inner joy, light, and warmth. You will not fill yourself seriously with any purchases; this is just some trick. As a temporary measure, as a substitute for self-love - this is possible, but you should not believe the TV, this is not the joy of life, and this is not self-love. This is a low-quality life, this life is not serious, and an intelligent man with such a woman will not speak for so long now about something good, good, real.

Satisfying one's needs is not yet self-love. Someone after this begins to love themselves, and someone does not. Satisfying one's needs is sometimes only a substitute for self-love when a person seems to be buying off gifts from the fact that he does not love himself. Of course, needs are different. If you really desire to move forward, develop, need to care for other people, need to be needed, or need to master any business with dignity, quality, then satisfying such needs, you will have more reasons to love yourself. You will have one thing to be proud of. If all needs come down to eat and entertain yourself with shopping or TV, then such a love of self is unlikely to be long-lasting, and one who turns into a pig is no longer a human being.

Chapter 5 How Famous Women Take Care of Their Bodies: How They Take Care of Themselves and What Their Routines Are?

According to Emma Watson, stretching before exercise routines that last anywhere from 15 to 20 minutes will allow you to easily perform the routine if you are running short on time. It does not matter how you prefer to exercise. However, we recommend getting started by using an evaluation method, or what we would like to call "the preparation phase."

You can consider the preparation phase, or prep phase if you like, as a warm-up session. You should use the prep phase to check how active each part of your body is.

There are three sections that these exercises focus on: the upper, middle, and the lower sections.

If you have already been exercising every day in your life until recently, then you might not have to try out the prep phase. You can still go through the phase in order to check your body's stamina and capabilities. But for those who are getting back into workouts after a break, however long that break may have been, or those who are exercising for the first time, we highly recommend that you go through the prep phase in order to evaluate your physical capabilities.

We ideally recommend performing the below preps on a mat if you have one. In the absence of a mat, you can still use the floor, but make sure that you are not feeling any discomfort from exercising on the floor.

Lower Body Prep

Place your back against the wall without bending forward too much. Now slide down the wall until your thighs are almost parallel to the floor. If you cannot move down far enough to attain this position, then try to slide down as much as possible.

Start the timer and hold the position for as long as you can.

- if you can hold the position for 90 seconds or more, then you can give yourself an excellent score.

- if you can hold the position for at least 60 seconds, but no more than 90 seconds, then you can give yourself a good score.

- if you can hold the position for at least 30 seconds, but no more than 60 seconds, then you can give yourself an average score.

- if you can hold the position for at less than 30 seconds, then you can give yourself a below-average score.

Final Result

Your score lets you know how much stamina and physical prowess you have. For example, with an excellent score, then you are likely in peak physical form. But do note that this prep was just for your lower body.

Middle Body Prep

This prep is fairly simple. You are going to perform as many crunches as you can. To do a successful crunch, lie down with your back to the floor. Fold your legs until they are making a rough 'A' shape. Place your hands behind your head. All you have to do is lift your shoulders off the mat or floor. Ideally, your shoulders should incline at approximately a 30-degree angle.

You need to do as many reps, or repetitions, as possible.

Each repetition consists of the following:

• Lift your shoulders off the mat (to the 30-degree mark).

• Bring the shoulders back down.

When you are ready, begin counting the reps.

• If you can perform 50 reps, then you can give yourself an excellent score.

• If you can perform anywhere from 35 reps to 49 reps, then you can give yourself a good score.

• If you can perform anywhere from 20 reps to 34 reps, then you can give yourself an average score.

- If you can perform fewer than 20 reps, then you can give yourself a below-average score.

Final Result

Once again, the final score lets you know just how much stamina and physical capability you have in the middle section of your body.

Upper Body Prep

For your upper body, you are going to perform a half push-up. How does that work?

To begin with, one of the complaints that many people give is they are quite unsure how to get into the perfect push-up position. This is understandable. There are so many recommendations from fitness health instructors that, often, people are left wondering what advice they should follow.

Here is what you need to remember:

• You should own the plank position. Ideally, you should be balancing on your toes curled inwards. Make sure you practice this, so you do not injure your toes while doing the push-up.

• You should start in the upright position, where you have pushed yourself away from the floor as far back as possible.

- Keep your body straight. We have seen people bend at the hips or the buttocks area and that is not the right way to do a push-up.

- Your arms should be below your shoulders, slightly apart.

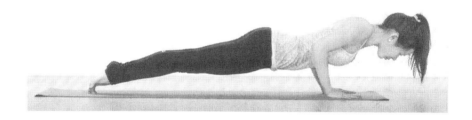

Image: Your arms should be below your shoulders and not below your abdomen, as some people like to assume.

So, what is a half-push up?

In a typical push-up, your knees are lifted off the ground. However, in a half push-up position, your knees are placed on the floor.

When you are ready, perform as many reps as possible. For a successful rep, push yourself close to the floor until your chest is just a few centimeters away from the floor (or mat, if you are using one). Then push yourself back into an upright position, back to the initial position.

● If you can perform 20 reps, then you can give yourself an excellent score.

● If you can perform anywhere from 15 reps to 19 reps, then you can give yourself a good score.

● If you can perform anywhere from 10 reps to 14 reps, then you can give yourself an average score.

● If you can perform fewer than 10 reps, then you can give yourself a below-average score.

Understanding Scores (And Why You Should Not Feel Dismayed)

We understand what it means when you can barely lift yourself on the 9th rep of your half push-up preparation. There is this sense of defeat. You feel as though you are weak and are probably not physically capable of going through any of the exercises mentioned in this book. Others might imagine that it is far easier to just give up and spend time in front of their PlayStation. At least through their video games, they have some sense of accomplishment, right?

Firstly, we want you to understand why the aforementioned preps were necessary. Picture this; you step into a gym and you spot some with beefy arms and chest that looks like it could deflect bullets. In fact, if Thanes (from the Marvel movies) snapped his fingers in front of this muscular behemoth in your gym, then chances are that the snap's effects would be nullified simply because of the pure testosterone running through each vein in the muscle man's body. This particular muscle man is easily going through 30 reps of weightlifting, each weight on the bar looks like it could be heavier than the average man. Motivated, you feel like you should at least aim for 30 reps of your exercise.

But that is the wrong way to go. Remember this rule when you are exercising it is not about how much you do, but how well you do it.

When you go through the preparations mentioned above, you understand the limitations of your body. Knowing such limitations helps you structure your workout plans. Remember that doing 20 pushups a day is wonderful. But it is okay if you can only do 5 in the beginning. When you keep repeating those 5 pushups every day, they eventually turn to 10 pushups, which turn to 15, and then you finally reach your goal of 20 pushups. The key point to remember is that you have to maintain consistency in your exercises. Set a time every day for the following workout routines. If you like, you can do all of them or choose one that fits your requirements and perform it every day.

Let us Start with Stretches - Warmups

Stretches are a great way to get the blood flowing and make you flexible. If you find yourself unable to cram a long workout routine into your day, then consider going through some of the stretches mentioned in this section. You are likely going to take just 15 to 20 minutes to go through them. However, you might require more time if you are still getting used to some of the positions.

Stretching is a form of exercise that anyone can master, given enough time. They do not have the challenges that other forms of exercises, such as weight training, have. But that does not mean that you do not have to pay proper attention to how you do them.

An important point to be made here is that stretching also helps you align your posture. Our bodies are remarkable constructs. They are capable of getting used to practically any situation, molding themselves to seek comfort even in uncomfortable situations. When you are bent over your desk, your body in a stooping position, then your body is slowly trying to get used to it. Which is why, the problem is not the body attempting to get used to new positions – it usually does – but whether it actually becomes used to that position – in which case the position becomes a permanent fixture in your life.

Stretching helps your body to remove those fixtures and gain more fluidity in its movements.

Let us start with a simple warmup stretch.

The Knot

•	Stand up with your back straight, your feet slightly apart and your arms by your side.

•	Your feet should be at shoulder-width; ensure that the bottom of your feet have maximum contact with the floor.

•	Tighten your leg muscles. This step might take a few tries to get used to, but it should feel as though your muscles have contracted inwards.

•	Take a deep breath and when you exhale, raise your arms to the sides at shoulder height. Your palms should be facing forward.

•	Inhale and as you take breath into your lungs, raise your hands above your head. Clasp your fingers and then exhale. Your hands should look like they are making an 'o' shape. You will not be able to make an exact 'o' shape, but that is okay. As long as you get the gist of the position right, where your arms have to be curved inwards and joined together on top of your head, then you are doing it right.

•	Your elbows should be pointing in opposite directions. When they are, pull your hands. It will feel as though you are playing tug-of-war with your fingers.

•	Inhale before you pull your hands, stretch as much as you can for about six seconds.

- Exhale and then relax your hands. Do this a couple of times.

Chapter 6 Do Famous Women Also Have Low Self-Esteem? How They Managed to Defeat Their Fears and Improve Their Self-Esteem?

What is the value of self-esteem?

According to Emma Watson: "Your self-esteem is probably the most important part of your character. This precedes and affects your success in almost everything you do. Your level of self-esteem is really your degree of mental fitness. You should be in a constant state of self-esteem if you want to succeed at the highest and feel great about yourself." Self-esteem should allow the individual to be more confident and more successful in achieving their goals. Individuals with low self-esteem usually feel inadequate and under different circumstances may not perform well. They formed inaccurate feelings that they are not welcomed or appreciated by anyone. Those with a healthy self-esteem, on the other side, will feel good about their life and then about themselves. They can and do things more efficiently; they can feel proud of their achievements and of themselves.

We will be able to enjoy life more and more by feeling good about ourselves. Feeling that we are welcomed, valued, and respected implies that we have a healthy self-esteem, and that feeling will be mirrored in our ties.

Low self-esteem is one of the main causes of broken relationships.

Developing self-esteem helps us in our lives to welcome joy. That sensation makes you believe you deserve happiness. This faith, the belief that you really ought to be happy and fulfilled, is very important to understand, because with this conviction you will treat people with respect and kindness, while preferring rich interpersonal relationships and preventing destructive ones. Too no self-consciousness may cause people to become unhappy, fall short of their ability, or accept abusive situations and relationships. Several findings indicate that low self-esteem contributes to stress, depression, and anxiety. Research shows a positive relationship between healthy self-esteem and many positive outcomes, including satisfaction, modesty, endurance, and confidence. In almost everything you do; self-esteem plays a role.

A healthy self-esteem helps you to embrace yourself as it is meant to be and appreciate life.

Could you create a healthy self-esteem? The fact is, there is hardly any positive self-esteem. According to a study published by the American Psychological Association, self-esteem is the lowest in young adults, but rises during puberty and peaks at age 60, just before decreasing again. Participants in the survey assessed 3,617 U.S. adults ' self-esteem. In average, during most adulthood, women had lower self-esteem than males, but self-esteem rates converged as men and women entered their 80s and 90s. During young adulthood and middle age, blacks and whites have equal levels of self-esteem. The lead author of the study, Ulrich Orth, PhD, said: "Self-esteem is linked to better health, reduced criminal behavior, lower levels of depression and, ultimately, greater life achievement. Thus, it is important to learn more about how the self-esteem of the average person changes over time." Your emotions are the main source of self-esteem, and these feelings are within your power. It will grow low self-esteem by dwelling on your failures and shortcomings. Through reflecting instead on the positive points and attributes, you can counteract this kind of thought.

Your self-esteem in the present is not just how you feel about yourself, but how you fundamentally assume yourself over the long term. If you have low self-esteem, day-to-day activities can have a big impact on how you think. A nice smile or a better day at work, for instance, could make you feel great for a couple of days. Or even a not that great day can make you feel extremely low. And let us face it most days are uneventful and dull, so staying high can be a struggle when you have low self-esteem! A good healthy self-esteem is focused on knowing what you are-know who you are and be happy, just like you are!

Argue with your "inner voice" to help improve self-esteem

We all have a voice inside our heads that is continuously chatting away. Commenting about everything we've done / have / want to do. And it reassures so rewards those with healthy self-esteem. The inner voice criticizes us with poor self-esteem, sets us down and stands in our path! Of starters, if you do anything-compete in sport or go for a job interview, and someone compliments you the inner voice might suggest something like "he was cheating, you were bad, don't bother next time." What you have to do is challenge the inner voice, then snap back with something like-" He congratulated me when I performed good, maybe I wasn't flawless, but win lose or draw I did my best and I'm proud of myself! "Arguing with your inner voice is going to improve your self-esteem, begin now! Remember, you are the manager, you are in charge, do not let the critic get you down inside!

Use Negative Affirmations to Boost Self-Esteem

A positive statement about yourself is a positive statement. Use them in a method for relaxation as well as by explaining them to yourself in your head every day. Ideally you would like to rest at least once a day and only make those positive statements to yourself softly playing some calming music at the same time is really good help!

Definitions for positive self-esteem affirmations: Who you are-I'm great I'm good I'm unique Who you're going to be-I can be a champion I can be powerful I will recover I will lose weight I'm going to do-I'm going to smile more I'm going to control my emotions by constantly repeating those stuff for yourself you have no option but to accept them profoundly! You are able to become those things, and the self-esteem increases.

Self-Nurturing to Improve Self-Esteem

For order to improve self-esteem, self-nurturing is important. Begin by physically taking care of yourself, eating healthy, staying in shape, and obtaining all the rest you want-not too much and not too little.

To improve your self-esteem, self-nurturing makes you feel worthwhile. Regularly reward yourself by doing pleasant and enjoyable activities-especially if something positive has been accomplished. You have to be praised for successes! Think about the things you love about yourself and note them all the time. Do not dwell or punish yourself for failure-reward yourself in the first place for trying. Try to focus on the good and learn to forgive what you feel is the poor. Days when you do not feel good or optimistic are important, you have to seek things that are good for yourself, no matter how small they may be! Those things will help to boost self-esteem. It can be a great help to receive encouragement from loved ones to boost self-esteem. Tell family and friends to show you what they like about you. Tell them to be your release valve when you are feeling low and upset-this can be a huge help to boosting self-esteem by just listening when you let off steam.

The community is essential for enhancing self-esteem and preserving it is a huge factor of self-esteem that is surrounded by moist, loving people. Already I realize for a bit that is not true, not everybody has a loving partner or community network. Nonetheless, you have to make sure you are respected by those you have in your life, and you have to respect them for who they are. A feeling of understanding will help you realize that people's variations are all wrong. It will be easier to build relationships with others by understanding this. Bond to those you see and connect with every day, just speak, contact, display love, listen, be helpful, and be honest. Understanding that those around you think the same about you is a huge boost to your self-esteem!

Criticism

You are not sorry for who you are! When and when you are questioned, make sure to "judge" what is being said to you before you react for whatever reason. Do not apologies immediately! If the critique is valid then take it into consideration and respond by agreeing with the critic. If unfair, then, as with your inner voice, stand up to it. A well-composed and self-possessed individual will uninterruptedly listen to feedback and then react. Make certain to critique at appropriate times, it is often more difficult for people with poor self-esteem to give than to accept.

Before you "boil flat," do not let annoyances go, it is usually better to nip stuff in your bud. Be tactful and seek not to damage the self-esteem of others. Use the term "I" not "you," for instance- when that occurs, I have problems.

Self-esteem is generally considered as a subjective self-evaluation. Self-esteem is generally believed to be nothing but your own image of yourself. It is not outside of you; it is an internal thing. Self-esteem is about how we think inside and how we respond outside will be influenced by this emotion. Our self-esteem tends to define our personalities, defining our behavior, determining how we react to the stresses and challenges we face in our lives, and definitely influencing our interaction with other people as well. Particularly residing in a healthy environment for a relatively long time, positive thinking, productive actions, and feel-good experiences not only improve our motivation and growth, but also provide us with a strong foundation for our future goals and accomplishments. Thus, one can tackle challenges comfortably with the requisite confidence and maintain a high level of self-esteem. As a consequence, the level of satisfaction and confidence would be so high that ambitious aspirations such as self-actualization, self-improvement, and the standard of' ideal' identity could be reached.

Self-esteem is not an individual concept; it is combined with other important concepts such as self-respect, self-pride, self-confidence, self-dignity, and so on. It was never possible to separate all these ideas from self-esteem. As when we can compose alphabets, interpret alphabets, enter them in a coherent word that we can understand what it means, we can finally say we can read and write in English to some degree or to some point. Likewise, if we are able to make decisions, if we accomplish those goals based on our faith and commitment, if we are respected by the people, we consider important, we obtain a good position in our community, we believe that we are respectable human beings. Eventually, these emotions drive us to high self-esteem. In other terms, they have a lower level of self-esteem.

In this post, we concentrate on the environmental factors that have a tremendous impact on self-esteem. Although it is practically impossible to change one's climate, it is a reality that if we go into a different situation and momentarily switch our condition, we feel different. We feel scared / composed when we are in the company of outsiders, so when we are in the company of friends, we feel safe and happy. We could easily choose a better company.

Chapter 7 How the Lack of Love for Oneself Affects the People Around Us: Children, Husband, Friends?

Low self-esteem can be drilled into a child when either the parents ignore him or her, or take notice of their achievements, while harshly criticizing them for any mistakes they may make. The child feels there is no point in trying, and even if they do good, nothing will ever come out of it, so it is futile to excel.

Of course, it is not just the parents who are able to develop this most unwelcome function. Families are always, and often wrongly, an easy target.

One of the worst crimes of all when I was a child was conceit. That is why the contributions seemed to be downplayed so often.

But it is not self-esteem, nor is it self-love. It is neither pride nor envy. The Scriptures tell us that pride and vanity are deadly sins, and the apparent reason is that we and God cannot love ourselves. You do not leave room for other people or things if you are full of yourself.

On the other end of the scale, for example, if you are really a talented artist and somebody is staring at one of your works. Let us assume this guy, when it comes to art, knows what they are talking about and they are saying how good they think it is. You, with your complete lack of self-esteem, turn around and say,' Well, that's kind of you, but it's not really very good.' It is not just an angry response; it is insulting as well. You tell this person, in truth, that he or she has no clue what they are talking about!

"That's kind of you doing that. Yeah, I am pleased with how it worked out," it's perfectly acceptable. You do not sound your own horn; however, you appreciate your own ability as well as the expertise of the other guy.

Lack of self-esteem holds us in Do Nothing's lonely place. It can keep us from doing things that others love, so our hopes and goals can be ruined. So, is caring with self-esteem? Yes. So, what is it exactly? Here are five points of self-esteem.

An honest appreciation of what we can do.

Realizing our own values and abilities honestly.

Being fully aware of our capabilities as well as shortcomings.

Comprehension about our weaknesses.

Not being too concerned about what other people might think of us.

I guess this last is the most important thing. Not only can we be held back by ignorance of the viewpoints of other men, but these beliefs are generally unspoken. That is why I thought I wrote. Just look at how our imagination, in so many other ways, can keep us from achieving Healing Trauma and Stress Starts with Self-Love Your heart, mind, body, and spirit all need security and compassion. Therefore, in the cycle of healing depression and reducing stress, self-love is so necessary.

Your spiritual development and recovery will be hindered without healthy and caring support and guidance and self-love.

Your nervous system needs security to unlock trapped survival energy so you can enjoy life's pleasures with a cool, vigilant mind and stress-free body at last.

When you begin with some degree of self-love and self-acceptance, you are in a better place to allow someone else to support you overcome your pain and reduce your life stress.

Here is an important truth when it comes to true inner healing: true inner healing takes a lot of courage from you, because with the emotional wounds you will have to trust someone else.

For the strength you have built to try and overcome the pain and tension in life, please applaud yourself right now. You are on the way to a lot of happiness and joy. You deserve a life free of fear and anxiety.

Is it time for you to restore the nervous system entirely, because in many cases you are now guilty of over-reacting or shutting down fully, and you do not want to function like this any longer?

If so, just plan to respect yourself right now.

When looking in the mirror every morning when you brush your teeth, you can begin to increase your self-love and say to yourself,

"I esteem you." You can also make the decision to stop criticizing yourself. I realize it is easy for me to say that and it is difficult to do that, but at least it is my intention to start putting yourself down now. Harmful attitudes create negative feelings, which in the nervous system causes anxiety. Give yourself some freedom from your practiced conditioning, most definitely as a teenager, and learn new healthy habits of self-acceptance and self-love.

On the road to trauma healing and stress reduction, your self-love will accelerate your recovery and ensure a life full of joy and love that is your birthright. These feelings are supposed to go away while fear and anxiety are part of life. Such emotions do not go anywhere for you, so they sometimes get worse over time. The depression is not good either for you.

Anxiety disorders are the most common mental illness in the US, and you can now, once and for all, resolve this epidemic with all the modern stress recovery methods. Trauma is no doubt a lifetime prison sentence. It is time to celebrate and encourage yourself to through your self-love and recover 100% of your trauma. When you offer yourself this wonderful gift, the stress level will drop to a healthy level.

From Pain (Suicidal) To Self-love

Suicide is a permanent solution to a temporary problem, and this is what helps us to grow and become stronger people. Nothing is worth taking a lifetime, particularly another man or women. If someone has that influence on you, you do not have to continue with them in your life. Only suck it up, walk away, take care of you and be the person you can be!

I was in that position too. I looked like I was sick from a divorce. The gut-wrenching I already know, I-want to-crawl-in - a-hole-and-die agony! It was nearly paralyzing at times. It was not until some years had gone by and I could take a step back, that I started to see more distinctly how I played an enormous part in the split. Why? Because I saw someone who did not take care of themselves the way they should have been, and I took a good hard look at myself.

There was definitely a lack of self-love in my life at the time. So self-inflicted damage is not perceived to be self-love! It was difficult to see anything lovable about myself through the haze of pain. But I knew I had to learn to love myself if I ever had a healthy relationship. I will continue to draw unhealthy people into my existence if I were sick. All I wanted to do was get smarter and more self-confident, because a strong person is much more desirable than a weak person. So, it has to continue with me, otherwise I do not have anything to do with a new relationship.

Love yourself, be true to yourself, and prioritize your well-being. Spiritual, physical, social, and intellectual focus on yourself. Set goals and carry through at all times. Make positive comments for yourself. Surround yourself with people positive and uplifting. Do for yourself something good. For someone else, do something nice. The list continues and begins. There are so many ways to learn how to love and be content with yourself, and a healthy relationship is important.

After all, if we cannot even recognize ourselves, how can we consider someone else? When we cannot even respect ourselves, how can we expect others to accept us? In establishing a stable, loving relationship, self-love and self-acceptance are crucial first moves.

Note, love starts internally, and only when you achieve self-acceptance and self-love can you really express it with someone else.

Chapter 8 The Techniques That Famous Women Use to Overcome Anxiety About the Obstacles They Have to Overcome.

Anxiety can impair the normal functioning of a person as an unknown fear stays with the victim forever. Uncertainty becomes a part of life, and people start shying away from unbridled public exposure.

Most things that lead to anxiety are not real threats. It is the mind trying to put you into a protective cocoon. There are several ways to counter stress and anxiety effectively.

Ways to Deal with Anxiety

Mindfulness

Mindfulness is the phenomenal concept to help one remain grounded in the present. We all like to believe that we live in the present, but that is not correct. We live in a world identified with several things and memories to back that up.

For instance, if you are a successful person, you may expect people to greet you when they meet you. It is because you are identified with your position and feel that it commands that respect. When someone whom you expect does not greet, it kickstarts the thought process about the significance of that event. Normally, the greeting might not have meant anything to you. But because you feel so identified with your position that the absence of greeting might begin to look like a question to your authority. Thoughts and memories also have a profound role to play in this whole mash-up.

This event would keep running in your mind long after you have left that place. It does not remain a simple question of not greeting you anymore. It may also start creating self-doubt, and you may begin questioning your relevance and standing.

5 Basic Principles of Mindfulness

Detachment: It is a way of living that helps you in remaining detached. To live in this world and enjoy it, you do not need to feel identified with it. There is no need to categorize things as good and bad. The way we look at things can change the way they behave for us.

Non-judgmental Attitude

The biggest reason for our unhappiness is our judgmental attitude. We judge everything on the basis of our past experiences. We label everything and then make firm beliefs about things that can make us happy and sad. These classifications have little to do with the way that things really turn out to be. Mindfulness is all about experiencing things as they are without judging them on the basis of old ideas.

Living in the Present

Most people never let the past go. They hold on to the past very strongly. Due to this, they are never able to enjoy their present.

They keep working hard to make their future like their past, even better than it. However, they miss the present.

Acceptance

We have become very rigid in our beliefs. We resent any kind of deviation. Most people are never even able to accept themselves as they are. They are always in a constant pursuit to change themselves for an image that looks better. This attitude only brings unhappiness and discontentment. When you try to go against nature without reason, the results are never very pleasant. Mindfulness helps you in accepting everything as it is. Working for betterment is something entirely different but loathing something cannot be a part of the plan as it would lead to stress and anxiety.

Openness

Mindfulness is the idea of letting go of rigid ideas and opening up to new things and experiences. You do not stick to certain belief systems because you have been taught about it or have seen people follow them. You remain open to new experiences.

Visualization

Visualization is a great way to lower stress and anxiety. The main cause of anxiety is excessive focus on some negative emotions. It simply remains hooked on to negativity and does not allow you to come out of it. One major problem here is that there are so many negative emotions that they do not allow positive thoughts to come to your mind.

Visualization can be a big asset in such scenarios. It is a simple practice of visualizing something sweet and pleasant that you have always wished for but do not relate to it strongly. It detaches you from the negative emotions and gives your mind the required diversion.

You get a chance to visualize the things you really like, and they bring positive emotions to your mind.

It is a very easy practice, and there are several tools that can help you. You can listen to guided visualizations whenever you feel anxious, and that would help you in taking your mind off the negative triggers.

When you visualize pleasant scenarios, you are actually able to see them from the eyes of your mind. Seeing is believing, and your mind is able to switch tracks easily. Always remember that positivity is the only thing that can help you in the hopeless darkness of negativity.

Simple emotions of love, beauty, nature, and compassion can help your mind in thinking positively.

The scope of visualization is very wide, and it can become a powerful tool in fending off stress and anxiety.

Emotional Freedom Technique
Most people do not realize, but the cause of most of their physical and mental lies in the imbalance of energy inside them. We are

more than just the body. Our emotions, life energy, and physicality work in unique sync. Whenever any part of this system goes out of balance, we suffer as a whole. This is the reason most eastern medicine practices also heavily rely on energy healing. Healing practices like acupuncture and reiki can have a profound impact on correcting such imbalances.

Emotional Freedom Technique (ETF) tapping also works on similar principles. It is a technique that has been used to treat soldiers suffering from post-traumatic stress disorders, and it has proven to be very effective.

While for acupuncture and reiki, you will need to go to an expert, you can do ETF tapping yourself anywhere and bring down your levels of anxiety. Even in case a person is going to have a full-blown panic attack. This tapping can help in lowering the level of stress and anxiety and prevent the panic attack.

ETF is very effective, and it is very easy to perform. You can customize the whole process as per your need and feel your level of anxiety going down as you practice it in times of need.

ETF is performed in cycles. With every cycle, you will have to assess the level of anxiety you are feeling, and you can continue repeating the cycles until you start feeling comfortable.

Through this process, you address the negative emotions that may be contributing to stress and anxiety. By tapping on various meridian points in the body, you allow the energy in your body to flow more freely. This helps in restoring the smooth flow of emotions, and your mood also starts improving.

1 Single Out the Issue Causing Anxiety

There can be several things that may be driving you towards anxiety. However, if you will try to address all the things that are making you anxious at the same time, it would not be that effective.

It is important that you identify the strongest emotion that is making you feel anxious at the moment. If there are other stronger issues, too, you can address them separately.

You can enhance the outcome of the process if you address each issue in its own time.

2 Identify the Intensity of Anxiety

Before you begin ETF tapping, it is important that you close your eyes briefly and try to assess the level of anxiety you are feeling at that moment. Rate your level of anxiety on a scale of 0-10. It is important that you know the level of anxiety before you begin so that you can see the calming effect you are having and know the number of cycles; you will have to perform tapping. If you begin without scaling the level of anxiety you are feeling, you will face difficulty in assessing your progress.

ETF tapping follows a two-pronged approach. While the tapping helps in unblocking the neural pathways, the positive and reassuring statements help in making you emotionally balanced.

In the third step, you will have to establish a setup phrase that will help you in addressing the problem, causing stress and anxiety.

This setup phrase should simply have two main portions:

1. It must directly acknowledge the issue you are facing

2. In this statement, you must accept and encourage yourself despite all the problems

For instance, if you are feeling really frightened due to anything, acknowledge your fear in the first part of the statement. In the second part, accept yourself despite your fears and flaws and reassure your mind that you will come out of it.

Your setup statement can be something like this:

Even though I am feeling scared and anxious, I completely accept myself, and I will come out of it.

I want to run away from all this, I understand I am scared, but I will come out of it, I accept myself.

I am feeling lost at the moment, but I will find my way. I love myself and accept the feelings I am having at the moment.

As an individual, you can have your own setup statement that addresses the most important issue you are facing at the moment. Try to keep the statement simple and more focused. Also, remember that your setup statement should only have your problem as the center argument. Including the problems faced by others does not work here. It is not a prayer; it is a way to heal your mind.

4 The ETF Tapping Sequence

In this part, you will have to tap the meridian point explained below. You can tap the points from your index fingers or your middle finger or both if you like. Even if you want to use more fingers, feel free to do that. The tapping does not need to be very hard; remember some parts are sensitive, and it can hurt if you tap too hard. You simply need to stimulate those parts through the tapping so that the neural pathways open up.

There are 9 meridian points that you will be tapping in this step are:

Hand (Karate Chop)

This is the side of your palm below your pinky finger. The part of the hand used for giving karate chops. This is the reason it is called karate chop. Using the fingers of the opposite hand, tap on this surface.

The inner edge of the eyebrows

You will need to tap at the center of your eyebrows just above the bridge of the nose.

Side of the eyes

This is the outer edge of the eyes where the eyebrows end. This will be the part between your eyebrows and the temple.

Under the eyes

This is the area under the eyes where the hard part of the cheekbone is.

Under the nose

This is the area just below the nose and center of your upper lip.

Chin

This is the area at the center just below your lower lip and above your chin

Beginning of the collarbone

This is the area where the collarbones begin

Underarms

This area is approximately 4 inches below the armpits.

Top of the head

This is the crown of your head. The topmost part.

Chapter 9 How to Improve Your Love Life by Starting to Love Yourself More?

Be firm but gracious when communicating your limits with men. The key to expressing your boundaries or rebuffing a man's premature sexual advances in an attractive way is to allude to your desire for him while setting your standard.

Never be afraid to enforce your personal boundaries or express your limitations with a man. Being able to do so with poise and decorum will subconsciously communicate to him that you are a high-value woman, one who has standards and reasonable expectations. Women who can confidently tell a man what they want and do not want are rare and therefore VERY sought after.

Unfortunately, many women are terrified to set boundaries with a man they are highly attracted to because they fear that he will lose interest, withdraw, or become completely turned off. These women believe that telling a man "No" or shutting down his premature sexual advances might drive away a potential boyfriend. If you struggle to set boundaries with men due to a deep fear of potential loss, you can stop worrying about it. Your fear of loss is groundless, and here is why: The men who will not be turned off by your limits are the ones who will cherish you the most.

Of course, if you are worried about coming across as being "too demanding" or "not interested enough", try to use the "firm but enticing" technique. When you must express your limitations or outright reject a man's advances, simply state how you feel but use a hint of seduction to keep him intrigued. Here is a simple yet powerful step-by-step communication method for accomplishing this:

Compliment him by telling him how he makes you feel. The best way to do this is to say something genuine about him that singles him out as being "better" than other men in some way.

Communicate your boundaries and tell him "No" in a clear but courteous way.

Express to him why the boundary is important to you.

For example, if a man is trying to be too sexually forward with you, it's one thing to tell him, "No, I'm not ready," and another thing to tell him, "Listen, Mike, I like you. A lot. I mean...you make me feel things I have never felt for any man before. But I am not ready for this yet. I want to give myself to the man who wants me for a lifetime. I hope you understand."

Did you see the difference there?

The first boundary setting is perfectly fine, but it will not make his mind burn with anticipation and curiosity like the second one. And if "Mike" considers himself to be a potential "lifetime lover" candidate, he will do whatever he can to prove to you that he is the man for job, no matter how long it takes.

By using the firm but enticing technique you will communicate your limits and make the right man desperate to see you again all at the same time. Men do not mind being rejected once it is done with grace and respect for their ego. A man is less likely to see your rejection as a sign of your "lack of interest" if you can communicate your boundaries with a sincere expression of desire.

Never make yourself a fool for flaky male behavior. If you allow a man to flake on you once, he will most assuredly do it again…and again…and again.

In the event you are not familiar with the term, a "flake" is basically someone who does not follow through. They are major procrastinators, highly unreliable, and nearly incapable of keeping their word. The major factor in determining whether or not a flake will actually follow through is based on his or her mood at the time or the urgency of the need to act. In short, flakes make terrible friends and disastrous partners (both in love and in business) to those unfortunate enough to rely on them.

But what are the telling behaviors of the flaky male specimen in a dating situation? Below I have listed a few of the most common examples of flaky behavior a man might unknowingly display when interacting with a woman:

He becomes wishy-washy with his attention and might even break off contact with you as soon as you begin showing a serious interest in him.

He disappears from time to time or does not respond in a reasonable amount of time when communicating with you and does not give a valid explanation for doing so.

He cancels dates on short notice without suggesting a future date to make up for it.

He arrives unreasonably late and gives off an attitude of indifference towards his tardiness.

He defends his flakiness with the belief that he "doesn't owe you anything" and that he can "do as he pleases", in spite of the fact you have already made significant investments of love and loyalty towards him.

He does not follow through on his word and usually gives a dishonest excuse for doing so. That is, if he actually cares enough to provide an excuse at all.

Simply put, a man who flakes on you does not hold you in high regard. If he does not hold you in high regard, he does not deserve your attention. It does not really matter "why" he flaked, as men flake on women for a myriad of reasons that could span a book of its own (most of those reasons have nothing to do with you by the way). All you need to concern yourself with is how you respond to Flaky Frank moving forward. Once you realize that a guy is not respectful of your time and attention, you must cease to entertain him and turn your attention to more persistent admirers.

The high-value woman does not accept unreasonable tardiness without a reasonable excuse.

Let us say a handsome gentleman (we will call him Mr. Handsome Face) you met through a friend of a friend has finally asked you out on a date. Let us also say that he tells you he is going to pick you up on Friday night at eight o'clock sharp. Excitedly, you prepare for the date well in advance with some long over-due personal beautification and you even borrow a gorgeous outfit from one of your close friends (you know, the one who has ALL the clothes you like).

Friday evening arrives and you eagerly wait for Mr. Handsome Face to show up. Seven thirty rolls by and you are almost done getting ready. Seven fifty rolls by, and you are done-up proper and waiting patiently on your couch trying to read a novel to distract yourself. Eight o'clock rolls by and you are expecting him to knock on your door at any moment. Eight fifteen rolls by and naturally, you are getting a little over-anxious. Eight thirty rolls by and now you are getting a little concerned.

Ignore his tardiness and go on the date anyway.

Graciously ask for an explanation for his tardiness and then politely refuse the date if he does not have one.

Throw a drink in his face right before you slam the door on him.

As a self-possessed woman of class, I'm going to assume you went with B, as B is truly the only option if you want to communicate to a man that your attention is valuable and that your good-graces are not cheap commodities. Accepting a man's extreme tardiness without a reasonable excuse will go beyond him thinking that you are "easy-going", he'll simply think you're "easy." Not having standards or setting boundaries when it comes to your attention forces a man to make a value judgment about you that tells him: She is not worth my best wooing efforts.

Let us be real here. Being unreasonably late to meet someone or do something is basically bad manners no matter the situation, and thus it is not the kind of behavior anyone should encourage. If you consistently entertain such behavior you will find that people will not respect your time, which ultimately means that they do not respect you. The same applies when it comes to a fresh romance. If you begin making allowances for a guy early on without some sort of polite penalty or gracious reprimand, he will not value the attention you give him and thus, he will not respect you. And if you do not know by now, a man will not commit his all to a woman if he does not respect her.

Do not tolerate men who show indifference towards your tender display of emotions. Use your emotional vulnerabilities to test a man's compassion, esteem, and earnestness of affection for you. Only the man with a kindred soul will be drawn to you even more when you share your soul with him.

One of the most effective things you can do to determine if a man is genuinely interested in you is to share your vulnerable side with him, then observe how he responds to you (assuming he responds at all). Of course, you do not have to confess your deepest darkest secrets to him, but instead, share private little intimacies with him that you would not share with the average person. Such private merriments and concerns may include but are not limited to:

Cherished childhood memories.

Painful memories from your past, such as a friend's betrayal.

Present-day struggles, such as your fear of switching careers or the issues you are having with a co-worker.

Quirky interests that you are passionate (or obsessed) about.

Things that make you deeply emotional in any way, such as mistreated pets, domestic violence, your church's ministry, or your sister's rehab journey.

If you open up about such things and Mr. Tall-Dark-and-Handsome does not appear even remotely interested, moved, or engaged with what you're saying, he's probably not as into you as you would have hoped. When a man has a sincere romantic interest in a woman, he will not be able to hide his sympathies and enthusiasms whenever she shares the beautiful varieties of her emotions with him.

Truth is, getting emotional with the man you are dating will either frighten him away (Mr. Wrong) or draw him closer to you (Mr. Right), so you cannot lose with this strategy. Becoming vulnerable with a guy allows him to catch glimpses of your soul. And if he is Mr. Right he will become even more curious and infatuated with you over time. He will see you as a "kindred soul" so to speak and will feel even more emotionally drawn to you in the process.

Now, my only caveat with this approach is to be sure that you are only showing 'glimpses' into your soul. Things can easily backfire if you spew out the contents of your heart all in one go. Doing so can potentially frighten guys away if you are not discerning with your approach. You want to reveal just enough of your heart to see if he can engage with you on an emotional level, but not so much that he feels overwhelmed all at once.

Chapter 10   How to Become More Seductive by Loving Yourself More

All of these factors combined make up what I believe to be self-love and if you want to learn to love yourself, you will need to learn and develop each of these components to healthy levels. Since my aim in this book is to try to teach you how to love yourself correctly, I want you to understand what you need to have in order to be able to completely love yourself.

Self-Esteem

In the simplest of terms, self-esteem is generally what you think of yourself. It can be said that confident people have a high degree of self-esteem while those lacking in confidence have low self-esteem. It usually develops through a combination of upbringing and personal experiences that shapes the way we view ourselves.

Most kids who grow up with loving parents initially develop a high level of self-esteem because parents would always tend to complement their child regardless of their actual abilities. It is the same with society in general. Normal adults always praise children and are generally encouraging. No reasonable person would think to give a child negative criticism.

As a result, we as children have a high-level of self-esteem because most of the feedback, we get is positive and adults try to be as kind to us as they can. As we grow up, the feedback we are given becomes more honest and our view of ourselves start to shift into a more realistic one.

Self-Esteem is dynamic. It changes depending on a person's status and perception of themselves. During times of failure, self-esteem normally goes down because we generally also receive negative feedback while in periods of success, self-esteem goes up because the feedback we get is also positive. It is your evaluation of yourself, based on the feedback you get.

It is not always grounded in reality, and it can be subject to changes in a person's condition or social environment. It is also a result of the accumulation of the experiences and affirmations that we have had since childhood which builds an image in our minds about who and what we are and where we ideally should stand in the social order.

Self-confidence

Self-confidence generally refers to your faith in your abilities. It develops from awareness or at least a perception of what you are capable of. For example, if you believe that you are terrible at math, then your confidence in tackling mathematical problems will naturally be low. If you think that you are a terrible dancer, then you would tend to avoid dancing-related activities.

Like I said earlier, it is about your faith in your abilities and is not always tied to reality. You can be confident about your singing abilities because you believe that you have a golden voice while in reality other people who hear you sing think the opposite. Because of your misguided confidence in your singing abilities, you might be inclined to actively promote yourself as a singer regardless of what your actual voice quality really is.

If you ever watch talent shows on TV, you will see a lot of people who have a high level of confidence in their abilities. They view themselves as extremely talented and try to impress the judges and audience only to be disappointed when they do not win or even get angry if they receive a fair criticism from the judges.

It is because self-confidence does not necessarily reflect your actual abilities but instead reflects what you think of your abilities. It is similar to self-esteem in that it usually comes from your upbringing and personal experiences, but it differs from it by being more specific. You usually develop your confidence in particular abilities because of the feedback you have received whenever you display these abilities.

When I was little, I used to like singing in public. I used to sing at school presentations and I really thought I had a great voice because my parents would always compliment me whenever I sang. During school presentations, the audience would clap after I sing and of course they did, what kind of adult would tell a child that their voice was terrible? This made me confident about my singing abilities.

When I grew up and started hanging out with people other than my parents, I started getting feedback that was not always positive whenever I sing. Unfortunately, people become more honest in their feedback when you are no longer a child, so I lost confidence in my singing. While I still love to sing, I am no longer that confident about it that I would never sing on stage with an audience unless I was really forced to do it.

Self-Acceptance

Self-Acceptance, on the other hand, is when you learn to accept yourself for what you are. It is when you forgive yourself for all your faults and failures. It is when you appreciate your individuality regardless of how others perceive you. It is close to self-love as having self-acceptance means recognizing your flaws and knowing all your negative traits but still appreciate yourself.

Unlike self-esteem and self-confidence which are generally affected by other people's feedback, self-acceptance is something you attain despite the feedback you get. It is internal and more of a conscious choice rather than something that easily changes depending on what other people think.

When you learn to accept yourself, you do not judge yourself, and you do not compare yourself to others. It is being aware that you have specific weaknesses, but you do not let the awareness of these weaknesses bring down your opinion of yourself.

It is accepting your limitations as a human being. It is recognizing that you are not perfect, you make mistakes and you are not good at everything but still be okay with it. In other words, it is being content with yourself.

Self-Awareness

Self-awareness is similar to self-acceptance in the sense that it is the acknowledgment of your traits. It is about recognizing the changes in your emotions as they happen and exerting a degree of control of your actions following these emotional changes. It is understanding how these emotions affect your thought processes and knowing how you act in response to these emotions.

Having self-awareness is also similar to self-acceptance in that it is also about having an accurate assessment of your own weaknesses and limitations, but unlike self-acceptance, it is more about knowing how these weaknesses and limitations affect the world around you. Basically, it is about knowing how to control your own behavior despite your emotions instead of letting your emotions control how you behave.

It is like the idea of professionalism. You act according to how you are supposed to in order to get the job done correctly, regardless of how you feel about your boss or your coworkers. You treat your boss and your coworkers with respect despite feeling intense dislike for them because you understand that you need to cooperate with them in order to get the job done.

Having self-awareness means understanding that your emotional state can affect your performance and behavior. It is knowing how to interact with your environment and other people in a morally acceptable manner despite your emotional state. Having self-awareness means that you know how to control yourself.

Self-Respect

In simple terms, having self-respect means having pride in yourself and as a result, you behave in such a way that upholds your sense of honor and dignity. It is sometimes easy to confuse having a high degree of self-esteem or confidence with a high level of self-respect, but unlike self-esteem, having self-respect does not mean simply having a high opinion of yourself.

It is knowing what you are worth. It is having reasonable standards for yourself and behaving according to those standards. You do not settle for less because you know how much your worth and you do not hesitate to ask for what you deserve.

You are probably familiar with the phrase "Don't sink to their level" right? Having self-respect means exactly that. It means not compromising your own standards for anyone, even if they do not have any standards. It is about valuing yourself and because you value yourself, you do not let other people treat you any less no matter who they are.

Having self-respect also means that you have integrity. Your standards apply regardless of the situation. You do not bend your own rules or lower your standards just because it is easier to do so in certain situations.

If you have self-respect, you do not feel the need to beg for anyone's approval because for you, just knowing your own worth is all the approval you need. Basically, self-respect combines the elements of self-esteem, self-acceptance, and self-awareness in that you have a reasonable opinion of yourself, you are aware of your weaknesses and limitations, and you keep your actions within an acceptable moral standard.

It means knowing who and what you are and taking responsibility for your actions. It means that you feel worthy of being loved and accepted by others. It is acting with honor and dignity because you know that you deserve to be treated with respect.

It also means knowing how to properly ask for what you deserve and standing up for yourself if you are not treated with respect. You do not allow other people to give you less than what you ask for and you do not let other people disrespect you.

As a result, having self-respect means you also treat others with the same level of respect because you know that treating other people poorly demeans you. Having self-respect also tends to make other people treat you with respect because they see that you have standards and that you behave according to your own standards.

Personal Empowerment

Personal empowerment is taking control of your life in a positive way. It is taking all the above factors in order to determine your own worth and then using everything you know about yourself to set realistic goals and using your abilities to achieve them. It is knowing your weaknesses and aiming to improve on them, and it is knowing your strengths and using them to advance yourself.

Having personal empowerment means knowing how to take control of your circumstances in order to achieve your personal goals. It is also about understanding your own strengths and weaknesses well, making you better equipped in dealing with any problems that you encounter. You know how to recognize opportunities and know how to take advantage of them appropriately in order to succeed.

It does not simply mean having the power to make things happen. It also means knowing how to set realistic goals and having the freedom and the ability to make conscious decisions and taking the appropriate actions in order to achieve these goals.

Chapter 11   What Is Narcissism?

There is more to narcissism than having an inflated sense of self and being conceited and egotistical. Yes, these are all unattractive qualities when they are in the extreme; however, true narcissism involves a maniacal pursuit of praise, ambition, and gratification. Those who suffer from the slightest degree of NPD can be arrogant, smug, and vain and have an unusually high level of self-esteem. This is their outward appearance, but deep down they are extremely insecure and feel as if they have little self-worth. They thrive off admiration from others, which is how they feed their belief that they are more important than anyone else. Psychologists refer to this as "narcissistic supply," and it is almost like a drug for the narcissist. They are addicted to receiving confirmation that they are indeed superior beings. Typically, narcissists do not have an empathetic bone in their body, which basically means that they do not have a care in the world for anyone apart from themselves.

There are different degrees of narcissism; in fact, psychologists believe that we are all slightly narcissistic. It is even possible that narcissism is required as a method of survival in the world today. Being a little egotistical can be beneficial; however, the behavior of a fully narcissistic individual is very destructive.

According to the Diagnostic and Statistical Manual of Mental Disorders, to be considered narcissistic, a person's behavior must fall into the following categories:

- They blow situations out of proportion and are incapable of putting things into perspective.

- The narcissist is unable to empathize with the feelings or thoughts of others.

- The narcissist is only concerned with their own issues.

- The narcissist has no respect for authority.

- Deep down the narcissist feels inferior and will compensate by doing everything they can to be seen as superior.

- The narcissist is incapable of receiving constructive criticism.

- The narcissist needs sexual admiration and is often an exhibitionist.

- The narcissist is vain, exploitative, and dependent on others.

To a certain degree, all people who have been diagnosed with NPD exhibit these traits. However, there are also other types of narcissistic behaviors. Since the 1950s, there has been a dramatic increase in the number of people who suffer from narcissism. During this time, therapists have noticed that there are variations in the condition, which have been divided into several categories. Narcissism in children is typically a result of learned behavior from their primary caregivers and can be unlearned. Therefore, psychologists are reluctant to diagnose children with NPD. Fully-fledged NPD only exists in adults and is treated differently; other types of narcissism include the following.

- The Phallic Narcissist: These are typically males who have a great love for themselves and their physical bodies. They strut like roosters and are very aggressive and athletic. They are exhibitionists who enjoy putting their bodies on display.

- The Manipulative Narcissist: They enjoy manipulating and influencing others. The manipulative narcissist feeds their need for power by manipulating, bullying, lying, and intimidating others.

- The Paranoid Narcissist: The paranoid narcissist suffers from a deep self-hatred; they project this onto others with extreme jealous behavior, and they are overly sensitive to criticism.

- The Craving Narcissist: Although narcissists are extremely egotistical, craving narcissists are very needy, demanding of love, emotionally clingy, and attention-seeking.

The most significant personality trait of a narcissist is grandiosity. This is not the same as boasting or pitifulness, it is an unrealistic inflated sense of self. If a person will not stop going on about how they were the MVP of their college basketball team at a dinner party, it might show that that individual is boastful, conceited, or even a little ill-mannered. This can be extremely annoying; however, it is not narcissistic if it is true. But if the person did not even play on the team but sat on the bench all season, that is being grandiose.

What Causes Narcissism?

Babies are born selfish—it is natural. Their number one concern is getting their immediate needs met and that is it. They have zero understanding of other people's desires and needs. As they transition into their teenage years, this self-centeredness is still very much a part of their nature as they go through the battle to attain independence.

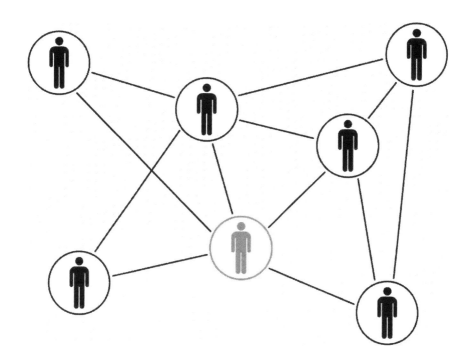

In order to care and protect themselves, children need to develop a healthy level of self-esteem, at the same time as being able to care about others to stay connected to society and family and avoid dangerous influences. When a child has a healthy level of self-esteem, it is an indication that a child feels that they are worthy and loved within their family and valuable to society. The essence of healthy self-esteem is not feelings of self-centeredness because the individual does not feel as if they need to trample on others to get their needs met.

There must be a transformation in childish self-centered behavior in order to experience sound mental health in adulthood. The ability to function effectively in a family, and in society is dependent upon the child's ability to gradually see other people's points of view and to experience empathy. So, an emotionally healthy child should eventually become sincere about the well-being of others. The inability to develop empathy as a child is a red flag that they may be at risk of developing a personality disorder in adulthood, and this includes narcissism.

Preteens do not have the mental capability to be manipulative, which is why mental health professionals are reluctant to diagnose NPD any earlier than the age of 18. However, there are certain behaviors in teenagers that indicate that they might be on their way to developing the condition in adulthood.

- Continuous bullying behaviors such as degrading, threatening, making fun of, or scapegoating people, including their parents and other adults

- The desire to win regardless of who gets hurt

- Constant lying, they will lie about the lies they tell, blame others for their lies, refuse to accept accountability by attacking those that report them to their parents

- A high and unnatural sense of self-worth

- Determined to get their needs met over others

- An attitude of extreme entitlement that leads them to act as if they should be treated differently than anyone else, and that regardless of the circumstances, they should get what they want

- Aggressive responses to being wronged, criticized, or upset

- Constantly blaming others when things do not work out the way they want

- Less cooperative and more competitive

The bottom line is that NPD is a result of the family environment that a child was raised in. All children want the attention and the approval of their parents, and they adapt to their surroundings. However, there are some home environments that are so destructive that the only way a child is capable of adapting is to become narcissistic. Here are a few scenarios to illustrate this.

Unconditional Versus Conditional Love – The Effects

Everyone wants to be loved unconditionally for who they are. If children feel that their parents only love and value them because they are special, this can lead to insecurity. It is impossible to win all the time, there is always going to be someone else out there who is better than you in some way. Children whose parents idealize them end up believing that they are only worthy when they are being idealized, if not they feel as if they have failed at life.

How They Perceive Flaws and Shame: Children who are idealized become ashamed when they realize that they are not the perfect people their parents raised them to believe they were. They cannot handle the fact that they have flaws like everyone else and so strive to be perfect in every area of their lives.

Unable to Identify Who They Really Are: These children are unable to get in touch with who they really are. They only focus on doing the things that will appease their parents and win their approval. They never spend any time exploring their true identity and discovering what their interests are and where their talents lie.

Occasionally, the golden child may resist their role and avoid becoming narcissistic. They actually feel embarrassed by the over the top praise they receive. The role that has been ascribed to them becomes somewhat of a burden. For example, one child of an overbearing excessive parent told his mother that he no longer wished to be a part of the circus and that he would like to live his life without having to live up to the expectations of his overachieving parents.

The exhibitionist narcissist parent will reward their children with attention and praise as long as they remain subservient to and admire the parent. These children are trained how to be narcissistic, but at the same time, they are prohibited from being in the limelight. The role they play within the family is to worship the awesomeness of the narcissistic parent without ever being critical of them or trying to surpass them in greatness.

This is how closet or covert narcissists come about, the children learn that they are provided with the narcissistic supplies of praise and attention if they refrain from competing with their narcissistic parents. If they ever attempt to be openly acknowledged as special, these supplies are withheld. The value they are given is based on their ability to act as a crutch to the egotistical nature of the exhibitionist parent.

As adults, children who were raised in these families feel too vulnerable, exposed, and uncomfortable to be in the spotlight, so their self-esteem and narcissism issues are not as obvious to anyone who is not close to them. Some take on the role and play it very well, ending up in a job supporting an overachieving exhibitionist narcissist that they have nothing but admiration for.

The Bottom Line

If you are ever concerned that the person you have met may have narcissistic tendencies, ask about their childhood and what their parents were like. Once you get a clear picture of their home environment it will not be difficult to work out whether they have narcissistic tendencies or not.

Chapter 12   Practical Exercises For 21 Days to Change Your Mind, Improve Self-Esteem, And Achieve Your Successes in Life

When you apply the exercises and steps you find in this 21-day self-love exercises, you will be able to discover both your outer and inner beauty and see what is truly magnificent about you like you never have in the past. You will become passionate about things in your life and when you are in love with the person you are today, you will find that your life is better in many, many ways.

When you have completed this 21-day challenge, take some time to look back on where you began just 21 days in the past. Chances are you are going to be amazed about how far you have come.

Day 1 Activity

Today's activity is simple, use your journal and write about why you feel as though you do not love yourself the way you deserve. Make a list if you need to, just be sure to put everything down that you do not like about yourself and things that you wish you could change.

Day 2 Activity

When you look in the mirror, go further than just saying "I Love You." Point out a great feature and say why you love it – for example, I love you (your name) because (reason). Do this each morning for the entirety of the 30-day challenge, and do not forget to jot your feelings down in your journal.

Day 3 Activity

During your shower, imagine it is Love, not water, pouring all over you. While this may feel uncomfortable or sound ridiculous, it is a way to begin to feel that love that you have been missing. Write down your honest thoughts on this in your journal and describe how you felt afterwards.

Day 4 Activity

Make two lists – one for physical and one for inner things you love about yourself in your journal. Review and add to these things regularly.

Day 5 Activity

Today, you will learn to forgive yourself. Use the steps above to go through each thing you dislike about yourself and write them down in your journal.

Day 6 Activity

Simply do something good for yourself. Do something that is going to make you feel good about yourself that you normally do not do. Get your nails done, buy a new outfit, or simply take the day to turn your phone off and curl up with a good book. Whatever you choose to do, make it something that makes you feel good and something that you normally would not do. Write about your feelings afterwards in your journal. Describe how you felt when you were finished, if you feel better about yourself, emotionally or physically.

Day 7 Activity

Put yourself before others. Let the universe know that you are important too. When you are writing in your journal about this activity, make sure to note your feelings. Did you feel guilty, liberated, and important?

Day 8 Activity

Write down memories when you really "rocked" something and the amazing way you felt. Add to these as you remember more memories, by unlocking these memories, you will begin to remember things that happened long ago that you may have forgotten about.

Day 9 Activity

Write as much as you can in your journal about who you are today and why you love who and where you are in life.

Day 10 Activity

Write down where you would like to be in the future and what you can change now to achieve this goal. You can also elaborate and add as much detail as you would like on how you are going to reach those goals and steps you need to take to get there. Make sure to add you fears, doubts and concerns and come up with ways to turns those into something positive.

Day 11 Activity

Make it a point to do one random act of kindness for someone by paying it forward. When you are done, take a moment and write down your reflections on it. How did you feel? Were they appreciative? Were you uncomfortable approaching them to help?

Day 12 Activity

Choose one place in your home, or even your vehicle, and declutter it. Pick one drawer, one closet, one cupboard, or the trunk of your car and get rid of the items that you do not use or are no longer needed. If you are choosing a closet, donate your old clothing to a Goodwill or Salvation Army store.

Day 13 Activity

For this activity, you are going to have to have some tough skin. Recruit your closest friends and family members. You can do this over the phone or in person. Tell them how you feel about yourself and the challenge you are doing. Ask them to give their opinions on things that you may be able to change about yourself that could make you feel better about yourself. Be prepared, they may notice things about you that you never realized and some of the things may not be wonderful and complimentary. Just remember, they love you unconditionally and would never intentionally do anything to hurt you. They are trying to help you and you are asking for their thoughts.

Day 14 Activity

Try something new as a hobby. It does not have to be something that you have to stick with, just give something new a try. You may find that even if it wasn't something that you absolutely loved in the beginning, at the completion of it, you might have found something that you are incredibly good at and makes you love yourself even more. Make sure to keep a list of hobbies you try and explain the project you did and how you felt when you were completed.

Day 15 Activity

Reach out to old friends. Reminisce about happy times and things you did together. By getting reacquainted with them, you can see where you started and how far you have come in life. Make sure to document in your journal about the experiences from your past, the fun times you had, as well as how you felt after meeting up with them. Are you proud of your achievements? Did you remember how you felt about yourself all those years ago when life was easy and fun? Write down anything that is positive.

Day 16 Activity

Relax and pull out your journal. Start at the beginning of your challenge from two weeks ago and read through all of your journal entries. As you do, reflect on how things have changed from the beginning. Jot down any additional items you want to add to the various lists you have made or make notes on how you feel that you have changed over the course of this challenge so far.

Day 17 Activity

Spend today smiling. When you pass a random stranger or are standing in the checkout line at a store, smile. If you are at work, and a coworker approaches you, instead of just looking at them and saying hello, smile while saying it. You will notice a change in how people respond.

Day 18 Activity

Graciously accept compliments today. Throughout your day today, whenever someone gives you a compliment, accept it. Do not let that feeling of doubt take over. Remember that you are worthy of the compliments. In your journal keep track of the compliments you receive today and write down how you felt when you received them.

Day 19 Activity

Spend 10 minutes meditating. Take the time for yourself to focus on your own wellbeing and to reflect on your good qualities that make you the wonderful person you are.

Day 20 Activity

When getting ready for your day, take the extra few minutes to put on makeup, do your hair, or wear that nice outfit that has been hanging in your closet. Throughout the day notice how differently people approach you and how you feel better about yourself overall.

Day 21 Activity

Love who you are. Spend 15 minutes telling yourself that you love who you are and that you are glad that you are unique. Highlight the personality traits that you have that set you apart from everyone else. Think back to things that people have told you in the past that they love about you. It could be your witty personality, your attention to detail, your ability to really listen to other, or even something small like the way you laugh, or how dependable you are. Write these down in your journal.

The first thing to understand is that emotions come and go. One moment you feel happy, the next you feel sad. While you do have some control over your emotions, you must also recognize their unpredictable nature. If you expect to be happy all the time, you set yourself up for failure. You then risk blaming yourself when you 'fail' to be happy, or even worse, beat yourself up for it.

To start taking control of your emotions you must accept they are transient. You must learn to let them pass without feeling the need to identify strongly with them. You must allow yourself to feel sad without adding commentaries such as, "I shouldn't be sad," or "What's wrong with me?" Instead, you must allow reality to just be.

No matter how mentally tough you are, you will still experience sadness, grief, or depression in your life—hopefully not at the same time, and not continually. At times, you will feel disappointed, betrayed, insecure, resentful, or ashamed. You will doubt yourself and doubt your ability to be the person you want to be. But that's okay because emotions come, but, more importantly, they go.

Chapter 13   The Nature of Emotions

Your negative emotions are not bad or useless.

You may blame yourself for experiencing negative emotions or, perhaps, you see yourself as mentally weak. You may even believe something is wrong with you. However, despite what your inner voice may say, your emotions are not bad. Emotions are simply emotions. Nothing more.

As such, being depressed does not make you less of a person than you were three weeks ago when you were happy. Feeling sad now does not mean you will never be able to laugh again.

Remember this: the way you interpret emotions, as well as the blame game you engage in, creates suffering, not the emotions themselves.

The positive role of negative emotions

Your emotions are not here to make your life harder, but to tell you something. Without them, you would not grow.

Think of your negative emotions as the emotional equivalent of physical pain. While you hate being in pain, if you did not have pain, chances are you would be dead by now. Physical pain sends a powerful signal that something is wrong, nudging you to act of some kind. It could be to consult your doctor, which may lead you to undergo surgery, change your diet, or increase exercise.

111

Without physical pain, you would not do any of these things and your situation would worsen, potentially leading to a premature death.

Emotions work the same way. They signal you to do something about your current situation. Perhaps, you need to let go of some people, quit your job, or remove a disempowering story that creates suffering in your life.

The fleeting nature of emotions

No matter how depressed you are, how much grief you are experiencing, or how horrible you feel at a given point in time, this shall pass.

Look at some of the negative emotions you experienced in the past. Remember the worse times in your life. During these most difficult periods, you were probably so caught up in your emotions you imagined never being able to escape them. You could not imagine being happy again. But even these episodes ended. Eventually, the clouds dissipated and the real you shone again.

Your emotions come and they go. Your depression will go, your sadness will vanish, and your anger will fade away.

Bear in mind, if you experience the same emotions repeatedly, it probably means you hold disempowering beliefs and need to change something in your life.

If you suffer from severe, chronic depression, it might be a good idea to consult a specialist.

The trickiness of emotions

Have you ever felt you will never be happy again? Have you ever been so attached to your emotions you thought they will never go away?

Do not worry, it is a common feeling.

Negative emotions act as a filter that taints the quality of your experiences. During a negative episode, every experience is perceived through this filter. While the world outside may remain the same, you will experience it in a completely different way based on how you feel.

For instance, when you are depressed, you do not enjoy the food you eat, the movie you see, or the activities in which you engage. You only see the negative side of things, feeling trapped and powerless. On the other hand, when you are in a positive mood, everything in life appears better. Food tastes great, you are naturally friendlier, and you enjoy all the activities you partake in.

You may now believe that, armed with the knowledge you have gained from this book, you will never be depressed again. Wrong! You will keep experiencing sadness, frustration, depression, or resentment, but hopefully, each time these occur, you will become wiser and wiser, remembering that this too, shall pass.

I have to admit, I can easily be fooled by my emotions. While I know I am not my emotions, I still give them too much credit and fail to realize they are just temporary visitors. More importantly, I fail to remember they are not me. Emotions always come and go, but I remain. Once, the emotional storm has passed, I generally feel like an idiot for having taken my emotions so seriously. Do you?

Interestingly, external factors might not be—and often are not—the direct cause of a sudden change in your emotional state. You can be in the exact same situation, with the same job, the same amount of money in your bank account, and have the same problems as always, but experience radically different emotional states. In fact, if you look at your past, this is often what happens. You are mildly depressed for a couple of hours or a few days, before bouncing back to your 'default' emotional state. During this period of emotional stress, your environment does not change at all. The only thing that changes is your internal dialogue.

I encourage you to make a conscious effort to notice whenever such events happen and start seeing through your emotions' trickery. You might want to go one step further and record these events in a journal. By doing so, you will gain a deeper understanding of how emotions work and, as a result, you will be better equipped to manage them.

Eckhart Tolle, the Power of Now.

Negative emotions are like a spell. While you are under their influence, breaking free from them seems impossible. You may know dwelling on the same thoughts is pointless, yet you cannot help but go along with the flow. Feeling an intense pull, you keep identifying with your thoughts and, as a result, feel worse and worse. When this happens, no rational argument seems to work.

The more these emotions fit your personal story, the stronger the pull becomes. For instance, if you believe you are not good enough, you may experience negative emotions such as guilt or shame each time you judge what you do is 'not good enough.' Because you have experienced these emotions so many times before, they have become an automatic response.

The filtering power of emotions

Your emotional state can drastically affect your outlook on life, leading you to act and behave differently.

When you are in a positive state, you have more energy available. This gives you:

- More confidence in everything you do

- An openness to consider new actions that could improve your life

- The ability to leave or break out of your comfort zone

- More emotional room to persevere during tough times

- Better ideas and enhanced creativity, and

- Easy access to positive emotions within the same emotional range.

When you are in a negative state of mind, you have less energy available, giving you:

- A lack of confidence that affects everything you do

- A lack of motivation that reduces the scope of actions you are willing to take

- A reluctance to take on new challenges and leave your comfort zone

- A reduced ability to persevere in face of setbacks, and

- A propensity to attract negative thoughts within the same emotional range.

Let us have a look at a real example.

Real life example:

Let me share with you a real example from my own life. Both cases happened under the same external conditions. The only difference was my emotional state at the time.

Case 1 - Feeling excited about my online business:

- An openness to consider new courses of action: I am open to new ideas or to work on a new project. I can think of ways to collaborate with other authors and start building a new coaching program to offer my audience.

- The ability to get out of my comfort zone: It becomes easier for me to push myself beyond my comfort zone. I may contact people I don't know or run 'Facebook Lives' for instance.

- More emotional room to persevere I stick to my projects even when I lack motivation.

- Better ideas and enhanced creativity. I am open to new ideas. I might come up with new ideas for books, articles, or other creative projects.

- Easy access to more positive emotions: I attract more positive emotions. At the same time, my mind rejects negative thoughts more easily, by refusing to identify with them.

Case 2 - Feeling mildly depressed due to my lack of results:

- A lack of confidence: I start doubting myself and all the projects I am currently working on. Suddenly, everything I do becomes useless or 'not good enough.' Thoughts like, "What's the point?", "I'm not going to make it," or "I'm stupid," cross my mind. Needless to say, promoting myself becomes a major challenge.

- A lack of motivation: I do not feel like doing anything. I am attacked by, and am unable to escape, negative thoughts. I have the same negative thoughts again and again, which repeat like a broken record. They seem so real and taint all my experiences.

- A difficulty to take on new challenges: I have little energy left over to leave my comfort and undertake challenging projects.

Chapter 14   How to Build Self-Confidence

If you want to be seen as confident, and reap the benefits that come along with self-confidence, you want to make sure that you are able to walk the walk that goes along with the talk. This means that you need to start building up the traits of a self-confident individual. As you develop these traits, you will find that you are far more likely to succeed in your interactions with other people. People tend to love those who are self-confident, and if you can manage to make yourself as self-confident as you reasonably can, you will find that your own positivity will attract more positivity into your life.

Believing in Yourself

Perhaps the most important step to becoming self-confident is beginning to believe in yourself. This is a tough one, as most people find that they struggle, at least in some capacity, with believing in themselves from time to time. Do not worry—you do not have to be able to believe in yourself all of the time. In fact, you should absolutely know how to tell what your weaknesses are as they arise, allowing you to tell whether you are actually capable of doing something or not.

Remember, a major portion of being self-confident is knowing your own abilities, good and bad. Even knowing your weaknesses and having a realistic idea of when it is best to completely reject the idea of being able to do something can be considered self-confident. For example, if you are being asked to go get something out of the deep water, but you do not know how to swim, no one is going to think twice about you politely declining and saying that you cannot—because you truly cannot. This does not mean that you lack self-confidence—in fact, it solidifies the self-confidence you do have because you recognize that your inability would prevent you from safely completing the request.

When you can do whatever is being requested, however, it is important that you believe in yourself. It is okay to be afraid of failing, but actually allowing yourself to fail due to inaction is far worse. Take the time to remind yourself that you can, and should, be able to do what you are being asked, spend a moment to walk yourself through the steps, and go for it. If you feel like you are entirely incapable of everything, then start branching out. Trust yourself enough to learn. Respect yourself enough to give it a legitimate try. Love yourself enough to not quit needlessly when you could have legitimately finished the project with a bit of extra effort.

Remember, you are more capable than you know. You just have to give yourself the chance to succeed. The bird trusted itself when it leaped from the nest for the first time to fly. The baby trusted himself enough to let go of the edge of the sofa he was holding onto in order to attempt to walk. You can push yourself over the edge and try to do things, too. Just believe that you can and give it your best shot. The worst that could happen is failure, and failing is rarely as bad as people think it will be.

Persuading Yourself

When you find that you cannot believe in yourself for some reason, it is time to persuade yourself to do so. Your self-confidence is based upon your own self-reflection and your ability to acknowledge your own strengths and weaknesses. This means that you need to be willing to convince yourself sometimes that what you are asking of yourself is not something that is impossible. It is not something that is even scary—all you need to do is give it a shot, and if you fail, you just try again.

This can be a scary one for many people—it is tough trying to look at yourself as someone that is capable after a lifetime of self-doubt. However, life on the other side is much more pleasant. Instead of being afraid of failing and letting that fear cripple and stunt you, you are using it as a launching pad. Everything was new to you at some point, and that is okay. Everything was new to everyone at some point—even the people next to you that you are comparing yourself to were new in the beginning for them—they started this life with exactly what you did: A blank slate. It is up to you what you do with that blank slate.

When you are trying to convince yourself to try something or to feel a bit more confident, try to stop and think about what you are good at. Everyone is good at something—you just need to figure out what that is for you. If you cannot think of something that you are good at, try some new things. Find a few new hobbies and attempt them. You will find something that you can take pride in—and you should. That pride will help boost you up into self-confidence that you can take with you and use better other aspects of your life.

When you do find those things that you are good at, latch onto them. Remind yourself that you have permission to not be good at everything that you attempt, but that you are also skilled at several different things as well, such as your ability to engage in whatever that newfound hobby is.

If you still fail to come up with anything that you are good at, try asking other people that you trust. If you were to go up to a loved one or a trusted one and say that you are working on your self-confidence, but really struggling to identify something that you are good at, you can probably get a few suggestions from those that see you when you are not paying attention. You may find out that you are actually significantly better at plenty of different things than you ever really expected, and that alone can help boost up some confidence.

Letting Go of Negative Thoughts

Negative thoughts tend to be at the root of all struggles with self-confidence. If you struggle to be self-confident, it is probably because you have all sorts of negative thoughts swirling around in your mind, and those can be dangerous if you let them continue to grow unchecked. When they grow and fester, you will find that more and more of your thinking and ability to rationalize your own abilities will become negative as well. Negativity is contagious, after all.

Think about the last time that you bought berries and left them in your fridge for too long. One berry begins to mold, and soon, that mold spreads and takes over all of the berries that were nearby, even though several of those berries may have been perfectly ripe still. Your negativity is like the mold on the berry—it will spread. It will begin to infect other areas of your life. Your one negative thought can slowly become two, then three, and eventually, using a negative thought process has become your natural state of being. You stopped trying to avoid negativity and instead unintentionally embraced it. In embracing that negativity, you discovered the dangers of negativity, and any confidence that you may have had will pay for it.

Ignoring Other People's Opinions

When you lack self-confidence, much of your life is spent worrying and wondering how other people feel about you. Instead of focusing on how you feel in your skin, you start to put your value in the feelings of other people on the subject. You want to make sure that you are popular, or that you are taking the road that most people would agree is best. You stop thinking about what you want or who you want to be and instead begin to focus on becoming who you think others want you to be.

Remember, the only person whose opinions of you matters is yourself. Ultimately, if no one else likes who you are or what you choose to do with yourself, that is their own loss. You do not need to live your life trying to prove yourself for other people that do not matter. You need to assign your own self-worth and look at that through your own eyes.

When you are willing to ignore the opinions of other people, you learn to be truer to yourself. You learn to embrace what you love, no matter what the consequence of doing so, maybe. You no longer see situations as ways that you could be embarrassed. An accident is no longer a mortifying event. All that matters to you is how you are feeling about yourself because, ultimately, the only one who has to live with you is yourself.

Focusing on Positivity

Finally, when you want to build self-confidence, you need to not only leave behind the negativity but also to focus on the positivity. Stop worrying about what went wrong—accidents happen. People are not perfect. Not everything is going to work out according to plan. However, you should be capable of dealing with the instances in which things do not go as expected. This means that you should be capable of recognizing positivity when you see it.

There is almost always something positive to be found, even in the worst of situations. For example, is a car accident that kills someone who becomes an organ donor and saves five other lives really all bad? Yes, the fact that the one person died is terrible, but there are five positives right there as well.

That does not mean that you cannot grieve if someone dies, or that you cannot be upset about something going wrong. However, instead of letting that grief or upset consume you, try to find the positives that you can see. Do not cry that you lost someone—be glad that you had them to begin with. Not everyone is lucky enough to have the friend, family member, parent, or child that you had, and you should think about how lucky you were that you had them in your life, no matter how long.

Conclusion

Possessing low self-esteem may result in people being discouraged, falling short of their ability, or tolerating abusive relationships and circumstances. It can also be a symptom of pathological narcissism in which individuals can act in a self-centered, narcissistic, and dishonest manner.

Including academic and professional achievement in friendships and mental health, self-esteem will affect life in many ways. Nevertheless, self-esteem is not an immutable characteristic; both personal and professional achievements and failures will cause variations in self-worth feelings. Self-esteem has been shown to influence not only current physical and mental wellbeing and health-related attitudes, but also long-term health and wellbeing-related habits in adulthood. Self-esteem is an extremely useful tool for health professionals during their encounters with clients, staff, other members of the health-care team, hospital, and medical students.

Women with low self-esteem consider many flaws in themselves, whether it is real or not. They are too eager to please and win the affections of other people and not to offend them. They are also jealous of other women with characteristics and possessions that they want to have. They have an aura of animosity around them and have no excuse to be irritable. They focus on the thoughts and compliments of other people to draw an image of their worth.

Women with low self-esteem may establish an attitude of the survivor, which may find it increasingly difficult to see the future favorably and express themselves. The more a woman deals with chronic low self-esteem, the more vulnerable and depressed, she may feel when it comes to changing her thoughts and behaviors. She may be searching for people in her life that strengthen her negative view of herself and those around her without being conscious of it. It is a process to change how women perceive themselves, and some women may need a professional's support to do so.

All women have the ability to make changes in their lives and be productive. Little experiences may give great lessons for women. She should take the spackle and do it herself instead of asking for her husband or a handyman to patch the ding in the wall behind the bathroom door. Small successes make a woman feel good about herself and accomplished. That emotion will drive her to take more risks and grow higher self-confidence and esteem. Through behaving with control, people can begin to feel it. Women can also pay attention to other women in their lives who take risks and have a strong sense of self-esteem and recruit one or more of them as their mentor.

If a woman is ambitious and has a habit of contrasting herself to others, she may feel inadequate if she does not reach her expectations. This can have an effect on her self-esteem. If at her last work-related conference, she gave a less impressive message, her therapist can help her develop a plan to cope successfully with failures such as these in a manner that is not conflicting with her self-worth. A woman sees hundreds, if not thousands, of other women who do not look like her every day of a woman's life, on the internet, on television, in magazines, and on posters going to work. These images affect how she feels about herself and directly correlate with the faith of that woman, chipping away all day long at her happiness.

Taking Better Care of Your Diet

Better health overall always starts in the gut. Your gut health is directly responsible for nearly every else in your body, from balanced hormones to proper organ function. When you are taking good care of your gut health, taking care of everything else becomes significantly easier. So how do you do that?

Proper gut health starts with a nutritious diet that is rich in everything you need to not only survive but also thrive. Eating a diet rich in color and with adequate proteins, fatty acids, and other important nutrients can support you in having stronger health in general. This means that you will begin to experience greater self-worth and greater self-esteem!

While supplements can be a beneficial way of getting important nutrients into your body, the best way to go about it is to eat a diet that is rich in what your body needs. Supplements do not tend to be broken down and absorbed by the body as easily, resulting in you simply passing many of the nutrients via urine or stool. If you do choose to use supplements in addition to a healthier diet, it is important to choose organic, high-quality supplements that will deliver the best impact on your body. You should also adjust your diet to increase your levels of healthy nutrients and vitamins.

Some things that you should begin adding to your diet to improve your overall health, specifically your mental health, include things like chia seeds, salmon, spinach, and eggs which are all rich in omega fatty acids. These acids are excellent for your brain health. Other foods include berries, nuts (especially Brazil nuts), oysters, yogurt, liver, and broccoli. These all contain high levels of vitamins like vitamins C, D, and B, protein, calcium, and other minerals. You can further increase your nutrient intake by choosing organic, pesticide-free food.

Exercising More Frequently

Exercising is an important part of our lives that many of us tend to overlook. When we do not exercise adequately, we begin to experience the side effects of this behavior both physically and mentally. Physically, we struggle to do things that may have been easy for us at one point. Perhaps we may feel like we are not on par with our peers. It can be more of a challenge to carry things, enjoy doing activities with loved ones, or otherwise stay active and involved in others' lives when we are struggling from ill health due to lack of exercise. Low stamina and increased instances of chronic pain are just two of the many things that people with a poor exercise routine face.

Increasing your daily exercise and staying on track with a routine are great ways to increase your physical and mental health. Physically, it relieves stress from your body and helps you get back in shape. As a result, your hormone levels balance out and you begin to feel better. Your body and brain function optimally, your stress levels drop, your strong emotions dissipate in a positive way, and your capacity to face things in your day to day life increases.

Receiving Adequate Rest

In addition to eating right and getting enough exercise, you also need to make sure that you are getting a consistent, high-quality sleep. Rest is a highly underrated part of our daily lives, and it is typically the first to be impacted when we are feeling stressed out or unwell. We begin to find ourselves sleeping less, feeling more restless when we sleep, or otherwise not feeling fully rested when we wake. As a result, we are exhausted, and our ability to function effectively throughout the day is further impacted. Soon, we skip exercising because we are too tired. Then, we begin to continue skipping it because skipping becomes a habit. Before we know it, we are also skipping eating or eating healthy meals because we are feeling too tired to prepare them. The spiral continues until we are in a rut, feeling as though we are at our worst with a poor exercise habit, an unhealthy diet, and an even worse sleeping pattern.

Instead of letting yourself get caught in this spiral that is all too familiar for most, you can choose to pay attention to your rest and ensure that you are getting adequate sleep. Whenever you sense that you are not feeling rested enough or you are feeling too tired to do things, instead of breaking your daily routine, seek to add some extra opportunities to catch up on rest throughout the day. Take it easy by letting go of unnecessary tasks temporarily as you catch up on sleep. Go to bed a bit earlier and ensure that you practice a positive bedtime routine that will support you in having a positive sleep. Using things like chamomile, lavender, and other natural sleep aids can help you resume a restful sleep. You can also lower the lights in your house about an hour before bedtime, turn off screens, and prepare yourself for a good night's rest.

Printed in Great Britain
by Amazon

43184213R00079